Up From The Cotton and Corn Fields Of Mississippi:

The Autobiography of Rev. Thomas J. McClellan

BaHar
Publishing

"To Deaconess: Dorothy Welch!"

Nov. 2, 2018

Rev. Thomas J. McClellan

FOREWORD
Up From the Cotton and Corn Fields of Mississippi:
The Autobiography of Rev. Thomas J. McClellan

And Christ said unto them, *Go ye into all the world, and preach the gospel to every living creature.* –Mark 16:15

After He was risen, Christ admonished His disciples to preach the gospel everywhere and to everyone. Preaching was central to His earthly ministry, and it remains the power of Christianity today. In His own way, God calls men and women to take up the mantle of preaching the Gospel.

Rev. Thomas J. McClellan received his call at ten years of age. His father was a preacher and pastor for 37 years. His mother's father was also a preacher. Young McClellan grew up in the corn and cotton fields of Mississippi where his parents had an 80-acre farm. He was educated in the schools of nearby towns—Long Branch and Durant, Mississippi. But deep in his heart he knew God had called him to preach.

Another Mississippi native, the late Rev. C.L. Franklin, had the greatest influence and impact on the life of Thomas McClellan. He listened to Rev. Franklin on radio every Sunday night. I, myself, grew up listening to this great preacher on broadcasts of his Sunday evening services. Even today he is considered an icon among preachers across the country.

Growing up, McClellan speaks of the tremendous impact of professional Gospel singing groups, including the Pilgrim Jubilee Singers, The Swan Silvertones, The Mighty Clouds of Joy and the Five Blind Boys of Alabama. As a young boy, he was frequently told he was a preacher, but didn't pay much attention to it. Still, at age 12, he drove his father to the four different churches he pastored, a different church for each Sunday, and McClellan began teaching Sunday School to his peers at fourth or fifth grade.

As an adult, McClellan and his wife relocated to Detroit, Michigan for better employment opportunities. Accustomed to having her hair done weekly, she found a beautician who invited the McClellans to her church, Greater St. Mark Missionary Baptist Church. The pastor was the late Rev. E. D. Kirby, who attended Howard University School of Theology and was the founder of Greater St. Mark Missionary Baptist Church. When you read his autobiography, Thomas McClellan describes that during his first attendance at Greater St. Mark Missionary Baptist Church, what he remembered the most was the request of pastor Kirby to escort "the preacher to the pulpit." This was the beginning of an amazing relationship, and the realization that McClellan was running away from his call to the Gospel ministry.

No one can boast that he made it on his own without anyone else. God brings people into our lives who are spiritually led to see more than we can even know about ourselves. Such people take special interests in us and help guide and mentor us in the calling God had for us from the beginning. It's only by God's grace that could account for what Pastor Kirby did in the lives of Thomas McClellan and his wife. At the time of Pastor Kirby's transition, Rev. Thomas McClellan was the Interim Pastor of Greater St. Mark Missionary Baptist Church. He came within a single vote of succeeding Pastor Kirby, despite his wishes that McClellan become the next pastor.

Thanksgiving Day 1986, the Holy Spirit led Thomas McClellan to Hartford Memorial Baptist Church. After the service, he introduced himself. I remember saying to him then, "You are a preacher, but you don't know it. Come here and I will help you." In the Lord's own time and own way, Rev. McClellan is close to completing a Master's in Divinity from Ecumenical Theology Seminary; he was granted a license to preach God's Holy Word and was ordained by the Progressive National Baptist Convention.

Thanks be unto God for His unspeakable gift. –II Corinthians 9:15

Dr. Charles G. Adams, Pastor
Hartford Memorial Baptist Church

INTRODUCTION

"Up From The Cotton And Corn Fields Of Mississippi" comes from a plethora of experiences and conditions the United States was encountering upon my entry into my family. They were the war years of this nation under the leadership of President Franklin D. Roosevelt. It is recorded in the annals of American history, and widely believed that 1940-1949 is America's best history. Yet, I struggled with the question: how could chaos, conflict and war between nations produce anything good?

According to the historians of that era, 1940-1949 was a good time to be alive in America, and for me to come on the scene. Whether that statement is conjecture or fact must be left to the historians. Here is what I do know: on March 14, 1944 at about 6:00p.m., Central Standard Time Dr. Brock, our family physician on D'Mathis Plantation of Edsville, Mississippi delivered me. I was the thirteenth child born into the McClellan family. I am told D'Mathis Plantation was in a rural village called Edsville, Mississippi located approximately eight miles north of Durant and six miles southwest of West. The plantation consisted of a cotton gin, a US mailbox, and a country supply store. Being the last of my parents' children born on D'Mathis Plantation, my father's mother spoke this prophecy at my delivery: "Jake, there is your Preacher and Teacher."

Following my birth, my parents moved to a plantation in the Long Branch community owned by a relative of D'Mathis; his name was Bros. Ingrams. My family moved to that plantation after my birth, and the last child in the McClellan family, a son, was born there. He was named after our father, Rev. Albert Lee McClellan. My father's family clan are descendants of General McClellan, a saddle maker during the Civil War in this country. My heritage is also multicultural; my father's bloodline is of Apache Choctaw, Irish, and African descent. I recognize and admit

7

unapologetically that our roots are in Africa, but our fruits are in America. My father's family clan came from Helena, Arkansas, which is located across the Mississippi River west of Memphis, Tennessee and northwest of Clarksdale, Mississippi. It may be of interest to mention that I share birth dates with a few notable people: one is the nuclear physicist and scientist, Albert Einstein, who gave the world the practical knowledge of nuclear energy and made it useful in the hands of well-trained and responsible human beings with the universal scientific formula, $E=mc^2$. Another is the musical genius Quincy Jones, a world-renowned composer and movie producer of Hollywood, California. Lastly, Stephen 'Skip' Curry, as he is affectionately known by his family and teammates of the Golden State Warriors. He is the highest paid point guard in the National Basketball Association. Each individual mentioned between the pages of my autobiography gives the reader of my book an overview from the time I was born to the current years.

Over the course of this book I have attempted to convey this message: don't allow anyone to tell you what you can and cannot do because speaking from experience, when you do, you will miss all your God-given talents and your dreams.

Thirty-seven years ago, standing and teaching my 8th grade Science class at Barber Middle School in Highland Park, Michigan I was told: "Mr. McClellan, you are a preacher and you should write a book."

I started teaching in Highland Park, Michigan December 12, 1979. My wife and I had relocated from Pascagoula, Mississippi to Detroit, Michigan on August 29, 1979. I'd started substitute teaching in Highland Park, Michigan in November of 1979, and I went to the Detroit Board of Public Education at Putnam & Woodward Ave. to file an application to teach in the State of Michigan. I was granted an official license to teach Middle School Natural Science and all subjects, as well as Biology and Natural Science at the high school level. The Detroit Public School District and the

Highland Park School District requested that I work for both districts simultaneously. Since we were living in Highland Park and I was already teaching at Ford Middle School under the late Carl G. Pettway, Principal and Mr. Green, Assistant Principal, my wife and I chose Highland Park Public School District. It was a smaller, closely-knit school community and they advocated and promoted quality education for their children, with strong parental involvement and participation. I and several other colleagues from Highland Park School District were selected for the opportunity to attend Wayne State University at the district's expense. I attended Wayne State University part-time in the evening after teaching daily, to secure a Master's Degree in Math Education with an emphasis on Computers. I obtained my Master's Degree in December 1991, and it was quite a challenge! True confession: I learned that running a classroom is similar to running a company. As a teacher, you are the Chief Executive Officer of the classroom, and not only do you have a responsibility and obligation; but with school, you are not only managing students as your 'employees', but also their families. This includes the student's parents, grandparents, godparents, and foster parents. Every day, you are creating challenges, teaching, and modeling lessons that will shape and develop their minds and characters. You are teaching students how to think critically and analytically so they can be equipped to overcome obstacles that were created for them before they were born, as well as those they will encounter on this journey called life. Do I have regrets? Yes...of course I do! Are you kidding?

For a large part of my life, I allowed people to tell me what I could and could not do. Being a product of a dysfunctional family and coming from the Antebellum South, it took me a while to process everything and learn that if anything positive is going to occur in your life, you must be the initiator. My wife and I just recently returned from our hometown, Durant, Mississippi. The town had been struck with a devastating tornado, resulting in one casualty. Multiple family homes had been structurally damaged beyond repair. The town is about 95% African American, along with other ethnic groups that recently migrated there. My wife family's roots are in a little town called Goodman, Mississippi just eight miles south of Durant. Both towns are located directly on old 51 Highway, which is very much an old scenic route in Mississippi, especially since the construction of the new interstate highway, U.S. Highway 55.

While we were there, she and her sister attended their old family church, Walden Chapel United Methodist Church. On October 8, 2017 my wife, her sister, and I went to my old family church's 131st anniversary. Their theme was: "Do Not Remove The Old Landmark" and my second cousin, the Rev. Robert L. Holmes brought the keynote message. It was my task to do the 'Prayer of Light' for the church and to introduce Rev. Holmes, the Under Shepherd of the church he founded, Mt. Moriah M.B. Church of Waterloo, Iowa. My heart was overwhelmed with ecstatic joy and the highest praise when the names of our parents, grandparents, and ancestors were called. From the original list of pioneers born between 1835-1935:

*Richard Rather
*Alfred Green, Sr.
*Wade Green
*David Denton
*Andrew "Jack" Johnson
*Robert Lee McClellan
*Odessa Young
*Richard "Tae" West
*Robert "Papa" Ware
*Will Smith
*Hamp Ellis
"Tommy Ellis, Sr.

*Charlie "Bubba" Horton
*Willie Green
*James Stovall
*Bonnie Turner
*Daniel Williams
*Isaiah Young
*J.W. Young
*Robert "Gauk" West
*Cleland Ware
*Doc Ellis
*Joe "Li'l Hamp" Ellis
*James McClellan

*Will Holmes   *Joe "Man" Stigler
*Rev. A.L. "Jake" McClellan   *Tommy Williams
*John Hooker

Do I battle with the ambivalence of clinging to old ways of thinking that foster and encourage doubt and fear? Am I yet disturbed by misgivings, unresolved issues, and restlessness of the past? The answer to both questions is an emphatic yes! And since my answer is yes, the ultimate challenge is: how do I change that? My friends, the answer is rather simple, now that I am a born-again Christian. I surrender all, daily, to the rejuvenated Spirit on the inside. I trust and believe because my faith is renewed daily through my efforts to develop a deeper relationship with the living God [Jesus Christ]. And I have found out over the years that holding onto unforgiving nonsense and worries weighs me down, when I can easily release the negative feelings. And so, as I travel this mundane journey called Life, I truly have to let go and let God. When I am obedient to Spirit, I feel a relief and peace that surpasses all human understanding.

We now stand on the shoulders of our parents and forefathers, as we navigate the uncharted waters of the future and wade through the wilderness of uncertainty. Finally, I know I have come to the place in my life where I am comfortable in my faith from all points of the square and the compass. I hope you've gathered by now that is a Masonic expression, but nevertheless, it contains much validity. My late father said it to me this way: "Son, by the time you get life all figured out, it's gonna be about time to leave here!"

I hope you know that, in all my writing and expressions, I am not rushing things in my life. But let me just say in bringing this book to a close: I would strongly suggest the reader to meditate and muse on 1st Peter 5:7. Everyday translation of Scripture: "Give all of your worries to Him [Jesus], because He cares about you!" And so, the releasing of my fears and worries to write this book was somewhat

11

easy when I remembered what my late mother told me on so many occasions: "The starting and completing of any task is a made-up mind!"

Are there thoughts or habits that I hold onto that maybe keeping me from expressing my highest and best self? Yes...but let me just say, I am learning how to let God have all of my burdens, my upsets, my blames, and my undoings. As I do, I am transformed to be more of who I am and was created to be. All I am trying to tell you is that it's a lifelong struggle on the journey of life. I promise you, you don't have to go it alone. I can guarantee you through a relationship with Jesus Christ and by letting go daily, He will give you peace, serenity, and love to permeate and occupy your life all the way. I have been receptive and open to the rich ideas the Holy Spirit has given me in the composition of this book. Therefore, I consider this book to be a unique and disparate body of my best efforts.

God's Blessing!

The Rev. Thomas J. McClellan

October 18, 2017

A SACRIFICED LIFE

My brother, the late Albert L. McClellan, Jr. transitioned this life at seventy years of age. He was approximately one month and four days short of his seventy-first birthday. He was the youngest child of the McClellan family. Our father, the Rev. Albert L. McClellan transitioned this life July 15, 1977 and our mother, Mrs. Jannie McClellan passed away on March 8, 1984. Three of our brothers and one sister preceded him in death as well; they were Phillip McClellan, Eddie B. McClellan, and William McClellan, and our sister, Inez [McClellan] Jones. Albert has one brother and five sisters remaining; a host of nieces and nephews; three children; and several grandchildren. I have chosen to write about the last two times Albert and I were together before he transitioned. I think there is a need for this portion of his life's story, because of the benefits it has not only for my family but for others as well.

Albert was a very smart and unique individual during his formative years. He was very independent and a self-reliant young man. He was a natural leader and a take-charge person by nature. He was rugged, outgoing, and personality-wise he was a lively individual. There is a two-year difference in our ages, yet we are polar opposites in mannerisms, behaviors, and our overall perception of life. My brother was a "late bloomer" when it came to the opposite sex. I believe he was past junior high school before he started to manifest an outward interest in girls. There were never any questions regarding his sexual orientation but unlike me, he just didn't display an aggressive behavior toward girls until after he had begun junior high school. And boy, when he did start to show an interest in the opposite sex, I mean, it was on!

My brother never was a jock, so to speak, or a lady's man. He never was a social, gregarious and naturally talkative person. He had a very unassuming, contemplative, and reserved personality—yet he had a vicious temper. He was very compassionate, sensitive, foreboding, long-suffering, and forgiving to a fault. He was very partial to those who were oppressed, suffering, unlucky, marginalized, and downtrodden in society. He was very gifted and scholarly in engineering, carpentry, building, and the sciences. I clearly remember hearing the late Mr. Eddie Logan, my brother's and my high school Science teacher at Durant Attendance Center, say how brilliant he was in science and mathematics. This was the local high school my brother and I attended and graduated. My brother's graduation was May 1967 and mine was May 1964.

My brother had a fascination and love for the country and farming. Unlike many people around us, our parents had an eighty-acre farm in the Long Branch community; our farm was located seven miles northwest of West, Mississippi and Durant, Mississippi. Following Albert's high school graduation, he purchased a type of high-powered Winchester rifle—something that would ultimately lead to trouble later on.

Now, mind you: he was so gifted in science during his school years at Durant Attendance Center his science class was summoned to participate in the local annual science fair. Several of the area schools competed for the highest prize. Well, I'll have you know, Durant Attendance Center walked away with the grandest and highest prize granted by the judges of the local and state Science Fair because of Mr. Albert L. McClellan, Jr. His science project involved securing clay out of the side of the road from one of its tall banks. After digging and securing the clay, he then took the clay and with his bare hands he shaped and molded all of the prehistoric men to their exact replicas as they were pictured from his science text book. I was asked years later by our Science teacher at D.A.C., Mr. Eddie Logan, who marveled in awe and astonishment at my brother's work—how did A.L. McClellan, Jr. pull off such a daunting task? He won the science fair for the entire state. A.L. McClellan, Jr. won it all for Durant Attendance Center in Durant, Mississippi.

Mississippi Valley State University offered him a full four-year scholarship in any area of science and mathematics of his choice; but he refused the offer. I want to write this portion of my deceased brother's life with honesty and integrity; not that I haven't already. I just want this section to have special attention—for obvious reasons for today's generation. All too often, our young men are misguided, ignorant, undisciplined, and uninformed about the ways of the world simply because their exposure and experiences are very limited after high school graduation. Generally speaking, young African American boys enter the Armed Forces with the innocence and deficiencies of youth; and so many find out later they have made a deal with the devil.

After graduating from Coahoma Junior College in Clarksdale, Mississippi in the fall of 1967, I enrolled at Tennessee A & I State University to continue my studies in Science. I clearly remember our mother writing me a letter requesting that I hurry home, because my brother had gotten into trouble with some Caucasian folks in the Long Branch and Bowling Green communities. When I arrived home our father was visibly upset! I began to make inquiry about our father's annoyance. As our father attempted to explain the situation I could see that he was visibly frightened, and he hastened to say that Brother was going to have to leave home; he had shot one or two of Mr. Connie Wilken's cattle. When I asked my brother about the situation, he naturally blew it off sarcastically. My brother had entered his late teenage years, and he was led by the testosterone coursing through his body. Naturally, he had begun to do things typical teenagers do during that stage of their lives; however—true to the traditions of this country—the dominant culture's perception of African American males as young bucks could easily put a death sentence on their lives. There are certain things you just don't do! The three of us had a conversation to decide my brother's fate, allowing my brother to be the key participant in deciding his fate. Our father suggested the Armed Forces and my brother took that option. Our lives were overly sheltered, we'd had limited travel experiences and exposure to the world; but considering all aspects of the existing dilemma and our parents' condition, Albert L. McClellan, Jr. chose to volunteer for the U.S. Army.

His basic training was done in Fort Polk, Louisiana. When he completed his basic training, he was later transferred to Germany. He enjoyed his basic training at Fort Polk, and immensely enjoyed his tour of duty in Germany; but the actual combat and war experience in Vietnam took an irreversible toll on his life. He was honorably discharged March 2, 1970. It was the Vietnam War that totally reoriented and took a total on his life and morphed him into a completely different person. When he was initially discharged I immediately saw it; but I did not know and understand the extent of the change in him. Sure, I thought that over time he would be able to snap out of the war years. However, he never did. Now, I will admit that if you didn't know him prior to his military experience, you would never have been able to accurately see and know the extent of the alteration in his personality. The devastation it took on him as a human being almost defied description. Now, he had an idiosyncratic personality; but when a person's life changes to the extent where he or she wants to constantly consume alcoholic beverages while you're in their company, that behavior is not normal. When an individual has gone through a morbid experience that he or she cannot talk about, that is a dangerous signal that irreversible and irreparable harm has been done, in my opinion. Many times, when we were in each other's company I would ask him about his Vietnam experience. Of course, I always respected his point of view and I'd always allow him to fully express his point of view. Simply speaking, even before his military experience my brother had an enigmatic personality. If you

16

didn't take time to truly engage him physically and spiritually during the course of a conversation, it would be easy to misconstrue or misinterpret what he had to say—and as a result, be totally confused by his presence.

By allowing him to totally initiate and lead the conversations, we got a chance to really reconnect during our last times together in July and October. We talked about a variety of things. He was deeply disturbed by an encounter he and our youngest sister had during the July 4th weekend. According to what he told me, he had spoken to his ex-wife in our sister's presence about some marijuana and beer in their car while traveling over the highway. They had come from New Orleans to visit him and our other sister that resides in Durant, Ms. As a result, our sister went berserk, lost all control and attacked him. He said she clawed and scratched him in his face, breaking the skin and drawing blood. He said his ex-wife visibly flinched, and responded by saying, "I thought you weren't gonna take that off your sister! I thought you were really going to hurt her, the way she disfigured your face."

My brother said the encounter angered him so deeply; he walked about eight miles up to the Truck Stop beyond the town of West in an effort to get relief from the anger of the encounter. To be totally honest and forthright, our brother never got beyond that encounter with our sister. He never told me the particulars of what occurred between him and our youngest sister; but I can honestly tell you, he never got over it. During our last person-to-person conversation, he referenced that encounter between him and our youngest sister several times.

He said to me, "T.J., I drove to New Orleans to see my son, Albert Gadson-McClellan, II." He said to me, jokingly, "I went by our sister's house and the front door was locked. Hey, T.J., I didn't even knock on the door because I was afraid she might call the police on me. Hey, man! I don't feel like fooling with no jail now, I'm trying to live now! I made it

17

through the jungles and the Agent Orange of Vietnam. Now that my pension has started, I am gonna get me a trailer. I don't want to finance one. I want to purchase it, because if I purchase me a used one, I can take it, cut it, and make it like I want to. But I can't do that if I finance one, because it won't be paid for. I want to put glass and windows in my trailer. If I finance it, I can't do that to it because legally, it won't be mine."

I said, "well, Brother, I hadn't thought of it that way!" His response was, "yes, man; when you finance anything, legally it's not yours."

Well, when I gave the matter some thought, it made good sense. Then he told me about an injury he had sustained in his lower back and right leg during his tour of duty in Vietnam. He recounted the story, by telling me their barracks were attacked by the enemy and they were running to save their lives. As they were running they came to an extremely deep ravine. They all jumped into that deep ravine. He said the man he landed on was already dead. He concluded the story by saying over and over again, "T.J., Vietnam was a living hell!" He concluded the story by saying over and over again, "T.J., I know for myself, God is real; otherwise I would not have made it out of Vietnam alive!"

He also told me that the Congressman and State Representative from Mississippi, Sonny Montgomery, visited them in Vietnam. Sonny Montgomery came to our parents' home at 122 Church Street in Durant and personally reported to them that Albert McClellan, Jr. was alive and well. Soon after that visitation, my brother was honorably discharged from the U.S. military back to civilian life. He had reported that my brother was alive, but what the U.S. Congressman Sonny Montgomery did not do was address the irreversible damage my brother had sustained physically, mentally, emotionally, and psychologically from the atrocities of the Vietnam War that had scarred him for life. Rightly so, he came to our parents and assured them that their faith in a living God had been sustained and rewarded through much prayer. He assured them, the parents of fourteen children, that their youngest had been kept alive. However, what he did not do was offer any financial assistance for medical help to reorient or restore my brother into the flow and movement of the normal American culture he had known before he left as an innocent young high school graduate.

I detected the personality change in my brother shortly after he was honorably discharged. In our last conversation, he confessed many things to me. But something he shared with me will always remain in the recess of my subconscious: he told he how he was permanently affected by Agent Orange, a toxic contaminant agent the U.S. Army sprayed on trees to kill the leaves. He also told me he had not slept in forty-seven years. I asked him how he made it through the night. He told me matter-of-factly: "I have to get myself a fifth of liquor or go to the VA hospital and get myself some medication." Then I understood why he kept himself away from the family; simply stated, I thoroughly understood why he lived the life of a hermit. Those last two conversations we shared as brothers served as a reconnecting point of where we had left off before he went into the military. He was very explicit, deliberate, subdued, resolved, and forthright on all the issues we discussed. I know for sure our lives are guided by the eternal loving voice of a God-life within. I am so grateful God had me in a position where I could not only observe his total physical being, but also hear and listen. Whereas Jesus spoke in the Gospel narratives often, He frequently began and ended parables with the command, "LISTEN!" I thank God that he had me in a place that commanded me to not only hear my brother's message with my ears, but also listen with spiritual understanding.

And so now as I reflect on our two final conversations, God had elevated me into a state of conscious awareness so that I could truly listen to what my brother said as well as what he did not say. Oh, Praise His Name...God had me at a place apart from the daily activities of my busy schedule in Detroit where I could go to Durant and focus on my brother's overall physical condition, with a desire to fully understand my brother's finite completeness and spiritual nature. And so, I listened to his final story using my divine inner guidance. When I got the news that he had answered the Master's call, the inner voice of the Holy Spirit connected the dots of our final conversations. God had me in a place where I could listen for spiritual understanding—for wisdom and divine consolation.

As I close the final chapter on the unbroken relationship that existed between my brother and I, I am convinced his life was guided by the eternal, loving voice of God-life within. That is why I requested the song by my brother-in-law, Pastor Charles Smith of Agape Worship Center Church in Kosciusko, MS, *"It Is Well With My Soul!"*

During our last conversations in July and October 2017 the spiritual side of him was very apparent. The effort he put forth illuminated his understanding and showed a level he had reached in Jesus Christ by faith and experience. The comfort level of his mind had allowed him to be confident in his growth, development and relationship with Jesus Christ; only he "knew what he knowed!"

It is almost impossible for pen and paper to adequately convey his thoughts and words as I experienced them through my ability and actual experiences. While conventional and practical choices can easily be made through this description of knowledge, spiritual understanding is not a function of the carnal mind. This understanding can only be accessed when one is prayerfully centered in the energy of the heart of God. And so immediately I was challenged, because I know this knowledge is not always specific. So therefore, it may not seem immediately relevant; it was not clear until his transition. Frankly, the Lord prepared my spiritual understanding to provide me with a feeling of His security, peace, and a sense of being exactly where He had positioned me to be: privileged to my brother's last testament of our earthly fellowship. Finally, I am grateful and thankful above measure for God's gift of spiritual understanding that guides me through every choice that is positive in my life. And so, during the last conversations my brother and I shared, in faith I know that God's power was present and operational and was greater than any circumstance that my youngest brother could have experienced at any given time.

Now I fully understand some years ago why he fondly and jokingly called me: "The Prince Of The McClellan Family."

Out of the night that covers me,
Black as the pit from pole to pole,
I thank whatever gods may be
For my unconquerable soul.

In the fell clutch of circumstance
I have not winced nor cried aloud
Under the bludgeonings of chance
My head is bloody, but unbowed.

Beyond this place of wrath and tears
Looms but the Horrors of the shade,
And yet the menace of the years
Finds and shall find me unafraid.

It matters not how straight the gate,
How charged with punishments the scroll.
I am the master of my fate:
I am the captain of my soul.

William Ernest Henley

IF

If you can keep your head when all about you are losing theirs and blaming it on you.
If you can trust yourself when all men doubt you but made allowance for their doubting too.
If you can wait and not be tired by waiting, or being lied about, and if you don't deal in lies, or being hated, don't give way to hating.
And yet don't look too good, nor talk too wise.

If you can dream and not make dreams your master, if you can think and not mad thoughts your aim.
If you can meet Triumph and Disaster, and these two imposters just the same; if you can bear to hear the truth you have spoken Twisted by knaves to make a trap for fools.
Or watch the things you gave your life to, broken, and stoop and build them up with worn out tools.

If you can make one heap of all your warnings and risk it all on one turn of pitch and toss, and lose, and start again at your beginnings and never breathe a word about your loss; if you can force your heart and nerve and sinew to serve your turn long after they're gone.
And so hold on when there is nothing in you except the will which says to them, "hold on!"

If you can talk with crowds and keep your virtue, or walk with kings nor lose the common touch, if neither foes nor loving friends can hurt you.
If all men count you, but none too much; if you can fill the unforgiving minute with sixty seconds' worth of distance run yours is the earth and everything that is in it, and which is more you'll be a man, my son!

Rudyard Kipling

THE IMPORTANCE OF EDUCATION IN MY LIFE

The founding father of public education, Horace Mann said, "An education is an equalizer in the condition of humanity and the wheel to social machinery." Being a product of the Industrial Era and offspring of an Agrarian family, this definition of public education resonates with me in a variety of ways. Education plays a significant role in my life now, and always will as long as I am alive.

While I was acquiring an education during my formative years, certain quotes from poets and other great people had a tremendous, direct influence on my life.

The late great Langston Hughes created a masterful body of poetry during my generation in the 20th Century that spoke of Black America's unique experiences during my generation and beyond. Also an author and playwright, his words pricked my consciousness to ponder how we, as a people, somehow remained so different from others after living more than 200 years under adverse conditions in America. One of my favorite Hughes poems asks the question, "What Happens To A Dream Deferred?" Even today, that question is as timeless as it is timely.

"How far you go in life depends on you being patient, sensitive, compassionate, and tender with the young and empathetic with the striving, weak, and strong. Because someday and at some point in your life you will have been all of these!"

How can I forget these words of wisdom by Dr. George Washington Carver, one of the most influential African American scientists? And how can I forget the late great Dr. Benjamin Elijah Mays, described by Dr. Martin L. King Jr. as his spiritual mentor.

Dr. Benjamin E. Mays was a distinguished Atlanta educator, who served as President of Morehouse College from 1940 to 1967. While Dr. Martin L. King, Jr. was a student at Morehouse College, the two men developed a relationship that continued until his death in April, 1968.

Dr. Mays was born in Epsworth, South Carolina on August 1, 1894 to former slaves, Hezekiah and Louvenia Carter. After briefly attending Virginia Union University, he transferred to Bates College in Maine, where he earned his B.A. Degree in 1928. The following year he was ordained as a Baptist minister. After earning his Master's Degree and PhD from the University of Chicago Dr. Mays served as Dean of the School of Religion at Howard University from 1934 to 1940.

The other scholarly, gifted, and deeply anointed person that had a major impact on my life—especially influencing my high school and college education—was the late Dr. Martin L. King, Jr. He challenged me early in my college career to focus on a non-negotiable and universal fact that is embedded in the dominant culture's protocol: a set of mechanisms designed not only to maintain, but to preserve and transmit core values.

The late Dr. Frances C. Welsing said it this way: 'The key to colors in America is a system practiced by the global white minority on both the conscious and subconscious levels is to ensure their genetic survival by any means necessary!"

When I look at today's generation and the changing attitudes sweeping over the United States and the occupants of the White House—including the president—it calls to mind this timely quote by an unknown author:

"But what a fool believes he sees, no wise person has the power to change or reason away. Ultimately, what seems to be is always better than nothing!"

This leads me into discussion of the person who had the greatest influence and impact on my life, Dr. Martin L. King, Jr. or African American. Let me begin by taking a look at the American Negro, or African Americans through the lens of Dr. Martin L. King, Jr.'s eyes. Dr. King said:

"When the constitution was written, a strange formula was instituted to determine taxes and representation declaring that the Negro was 60% of a person."

Today's formula seems to declare that we are 50% of a person. Dr. King further said:

"That same formula seems to declare a Negro is 50% of a person politically and economically...of the good things in life the Negro has approximately one-half of those of whites. Half of all Negroes live in sub-standard housing and Negroes have half the monetary income of whites. When we review the negative experiences of the Negro's life, they have a double share."

Even in 1967, there were twice as many unemployed; the rate of infant mortality is double that of whites. Here is what Dr. Martin L. King, Jr. stated about the statistics for the Vietnam war: twice as many Negro soldiers were killed in action as whites [20.6% in proportion to their numbers in the general population]. Of the employed Negroes, 75% hold menial jobs. Lastly, depressed living standards for Negroes are not simply the consequence of neglect; it is systematically orchestrated by the dominant culture.

Finally, Dr. King said,

"Economic discrimination is especially deeply rooted in the American culture; especially in the south. In industry after industry, there is a significant differential in the wage scales between the north and the south by design."

In all of this, Dr. King's efforts for social justice for this nation yet speaks in a loud voice.

And so it is said by Mr. Vincent Harding, the man who wrote the introduction to King's book "Where Do We Go From Here, Chaos Or Community?," and I concur:

"The glowing spirit and the razor-sharp insights of Dr. Martin L. King, Jr. are embodied in his book, "Where Do We Go From Here, Chaos Or Community?" The solutions he offered to the world, and especially this nation can still save us as a society from self-destruction. Hopefully, it will be seen and accepted as a testament, and the grief that followed his death will be transmitted to a universal determination to realize the economic and social justice for which he so willingly gave his life."

When I really think about my childhood as far back as I can remember, I was fascinated by learning about places and visiting foreign countries through reading. I have vivid memories of the neighboring farmers stopping me when we would come home from Long Branch Elementary School in the evenings.

I distinctly remember Mr. Tommy Williams, who would stop his mule team and sit in the plough handles of that old plough called a "middle-buster", pulled by a team of mules. He would ask me questions about my school lessons and call my teacher's name. He'd ask, "what did she teach you today?" Off I'd go, eagerly explaining and reciting what I had learned at school that day. I clearly remember the interest and enthusiasm with which he would listen and comment, offering encouragement and compliments.

I was astonished to learn later that many of those neighborhood farmers could not read or write. They had an uncanny way of making me think they already knew everything I was explaining to them. However, when I came of age and began to look back over the journey of my educational career, the Holy Spirit revealed to me that I needed to consider the time and circumstances wherein we were born. We were born at a time when African American people were a homogeneous family in rural communities in these small towns, cities, and villages in Mississippi. Simply stated, I came out of the village; generally speaking, all African Americans lived in similar communities during my generation. Regardless of educational status, our living conditions were much the same. Children were products of the community, directly or indirectly touched by every person in the village—in either a negative or positive way. These old farmers, many who could not read or write, had spiritual insight and foresight of the dawning of a new day and better time for us as a people in America; they were quick to show encouragement, especially if you displayed an interest in books and school. They wanted you to go as far as you could go and get as much education as your circumstances and economic condition could afford you, with their help through the church.

My father's mother invested in my education at an early age. She had a brother who was a schoolmaster in Paxston, Missouri. She always said I would be like him so she purchased puzzles, musical instruments, and various other types of toys at Christmas to stimulate my interest and mind. She even taught me riddles that I mastered and committed to memory. One of my favorite riddles was:
"I met Uncle Johnny coming up the London Bridge, blowing the bellow for the cat and nine-tail; whip Jack spurred Tom, through a rock and through a reel, and through an old spinning wheel. Sheep, shank, and marrow bone; such a riddle never known!"

My task after she had recited it to me was to memorize it and tell her what it was. Another one was: "Long Black Mama don't you cock me back!" She also taught me poetry: "An opportunity is like a bald-headed man with one braid of hair. If you don't catch him coming to you, you messed up with it pass." She also taught me:

27

"Man is a restless human being; you never find him satisfied. If he is allowed to prosper in silver and gold his heart is lifted in pride. He turns to God when trouble rise and fall on bending knees. But when things are going well with him he lives just as he please!"

My grandmother taught me how to pat a rhythmic, melodic rap called the "ham-bone". It is a rhythmic cadence between your feet, hands, and thigh, moving in sync with each body part, including patting your feet to create a unique sound that is distinct to African culture.

My grandmother really spoiled me. I was her favorite male grandchild of all of my parents' children. Once when I was about twelve years of age, I was hospitalized with a mysterious growth over my parotid salivary gland on the right side of my face. I must have spent two weeks in Durant Municipal Hospital. Dr. Brumby, whose medical office was in Lexington, Mississippi, took care of me and sent me home after a few weeks. Honestly, I don't recall what the prognosis or diagnosis was at the time. I do vaguely recall the nurses applying hot towels to that side of my face and eventually the growth dissolved.

It was the custom of the country schools to compete with the city schools in a yearly event called a 'Field Day' competition. During the game day, all types of outdoor sports games were played to generate the spirit of competition between the rural and city schools. The event was held yearly, around March or April. There were spelling bees, choirs singing, public speaking, and more for 7th and 8th grades, if my recollection serves me correctly.

The field day competition was held at Holmes County Training School in Durant. I was representing Long Branch Elementary School in the public speaking event. Many times before, I had represented my school in spelling bees at West

Elementary School under the principalship of the late professor King.

The late Catherine Green and I were always the two selected to represent Long Branch Elementary in any type of scholastic competition, whether it was for West or Durant schools. However, it was my assignment to represent Long Branch in the public speaking competition. The speech that I was assigned to give was "Invictus" by William Ernest Henley. When the announcer of the program called my name, fear assailed me, but it did not render me to where I could not perform. The problem was, I did not speak loud enough to win first prize. I knew something was wrong before I was done speaking, because my mother was in the audience. When I looked over to where she was seated I saw that pill box hat, the tightening of her lips and the outlay of that golden-crowned tooth she wore in the front of her mouth. I knew I had messed up! I did not win first place, but 2nd place in the speaking competition.

When we arrived home from the field day program my mother looked me up and down; her eyes examined me with x-ray vision. When she did speak, she said, "ole man, you could have won first place in that speaking!"

"Yes, ma'am, Mama," I said, "I did the best I could!"

"No you didn't," she replied. "Go get me some switches, I am gonna prove that you did not!"

She tightened me up with a few swats...to which I replied "yes ma'am...yes ma'am...Mama, I am gonna do better!"

She just kept right on working on me. Ever since she finished with me, I have not had any problems speaking publicly, or anywhere else!

Rev. Thomas J. McClellan
December 4, 2017

CHAPTER ONE

My life has its origins in the little village of Edsville, Mississippi. Geographically speaking, it is located in the hills of the state approximately 150 miles south of Memphis, Tennessee; 45 miles north of the state capital, Jackson; approximately 17 miles west of the city of Kosciusko; and 12 miles east of the County Seat of Holmes in Lexington, Mississippi.

This was a farming community plantation where I made my advent into the world on March 14, 1944. The primary natural resources of this village included lumber, cotton, corn, and some other resources. However, the resources that primarily sustained my family were cotton, corn, and produce that was grown from a garden and the fields. Of course, my parents were resourceful in providing numerous other staple crops that were in demand from the surrounding towns, especially for people that were not farmers. My older siblings told me that this village plantation community where I was born consisted of African Americans, and our primary livelihood was farming. The village had only a post office and a cotton gin. To be honest, I have no memories of the community at all; I was told by my older siblings that I was born there. Shortly after my birth we moved to a larger house called 'the white house' in a community called Long Branch, located between West and Durant. It was here my mother had her last child, my brother Albert, in November 1946. I am told by my older siblings that my parents had 22 children, and ten of us survived the perils of those impoverished conditions. When I reflect on the situation and circumstances under which I was born and grew up, I am truly blessed and highly favored, comparatively speaking. My family survived under incredible odds and, frankly speaking, squalor conditions.

By God's grace and divine providence, I have many people from the community in which I was conceived, born, and grew up that I owe a debt of gratitude. Many of them are not members of my biological family. I am sure neither pen nor paper will provide the space required to pay proper homage to these deserving and humble people. Some of them were my teachers, pastors, and church members; many were relatives, members of the community, and others were strangers and well-wishers. Of course, from my community there were a variety of people; some were destined to be farmers, and some were community leaders, civic leaders, lawyers, doctors, and yet there were those who had been consigned to mere survival by any means necessary because of their chosen and mental states. However, be that as it may, unlike today's community we were closely connected.

Growing up as a youth I encountered many types of people with many handicaps, or shall I say deficiencies. Many of these liabilities were physical and others were mental. I observed the love and the compassion exhibited by the church leaders and the actions they took to embrace the needy, regardless of their conditions—unless, of course, extreme measures made it necessary to take drastic actions to remove a community member. In the capital city, Jackson, there was a mental institution called Whitfield for people with extreme states of mental illness. My community was a microcosm of rural America, especially those that were of meager and minimal skills relative to a farming vocation. During my early growth and development, most of my time was spent doing chores that consisted of gathering wood, taking care of the livestock, tilling the soil for crop production, and maintaining the farm. My leisure time was spent hunting, going to school, and exploring my surroundings.

I don't have many pleasant or fond memories of my childhood; I just know it was vigorous, laborious, and time-consuming. I have to admit, I felt very little affinity for the farming life because it never appealed to my mental capacity, although I completed my assigned chores in a timely manner. There were many things I found interesting and fascinating on the farm, but many of my chores were not mentally stimulating and challenging. Consequently, much of my work was boring because it was routine in nature. While many things in my agricultural experience were mentally invigorating and challenging, they were beyond the scope of farming. I was fortunate in that the Creator imbued me with a curious and inquiring mind, especially in the realm of physiology, the anatomy of animals and in the other sciences as well. However, it was not mentally challenging in the least when it came to the repetitious pace of following a mule up and down the measured rows of a designated plot of land. I learned quickly how to adapt and adjust to my environment, if for no more reason than to endure and survive. More importantly than all the above, the land was not the property of my family; but because of the love of God, and the committed devotion and sacrifice of loving parents, we made it over.

Dysfunctional in our contents and flawed in our characters, it is still my family, and I'm proud to be of its progeny. One of the lasting memories I will always cherish about the village of my birth: it was a Christian community.   It communicated a special kind of holistic healing; special because it was completed: physically, morally, spiritually, and psychologically. In that community we were seen as whole beings. We suffered together with each other whether the suffering was of the mind or the body. Whatever the source, the wounds of the individual were those of the community and the healing was a forgiving kind, and shared by all in the village. One of the major messages of my community was not that a man or woman could be so awfully good; but that he or she could be so loved *despite* their failure to be good, and that the more they could allow themselves to be loved, the more their possibilities for good could be enhanced. Regardless of the imperfection that every individual possessed, the love that resonated and emanated from each person was so powerful and filled with God's spirit. Because each individual was so equipped and filled with God's love, it was impossible not to treat and hold each person accountable for his or her actions. Yet as pious and God-fearing as my community appeared to have been, it had its share of enigmatic, self-centered people. I remember vividly this community occupant whose daughter was my school mate when I entered elementary school. We were neighbors and I later learned we were distant cousins by interfamily connections. Her paternal great-uncle married my paternal great-aunt. However, as time progressed, we interacted, played, studied together in school and attended church. As we grew, boys and girls discovered at a fairly early age that we are inherently different from each other anatomically and physiologically. When that age arrives in children, nature takes its course without any help from parents! Having already discovered that we were different by nature, the natural curiosity of children led us to investigate each other biologically. Upon discovery of our inherent differences, curiosity took over; hormones had already been triggered, Cupid shot his arrow, and the rest was history!

As this young lady and I began to write each other love letters our parents became aware of our attraction. Now not only did our parents become aware, our teacher's eyes and ears become piqued. At that time, I was in the first grade; my teacher's name is Mrs. B.W. and she gave me an assignment. The assignment had a large chicken crate with a mother hen in the crate; the mother hen had a small chick, which was her offspring. There was also a large dog lying in front of the chicken crate with the mother hen inside. The dog asked the mother hen confined in the crate, "what do you do...and who are you?" Now, my mother dutifully and religiously taught me my lesson nightly as she sat me before a large, open-hearth fire in the midst of winter. But when I'd see our neighbor's daughter, alas, my lesson would immediately leave my head. So my teacher Mrs. B.W. sent my mother a handwritten letter. In effect, the letter addressed my behavior and my attitude toward my school work. My mother took the letter and read it attentively and from its message she decided a course of action that would remedy my learning distraction; she moved quickly. The course of action my mother took set me on a course of productive, progressive, and proactive learning for the rest of my life; even now!

In our front yard sat three large chinaberry trees. With the letter in hand she'd gotten from my teacher, she took me to the front yard and selected one of those trees. She directed me to climb the tree without shoes and get the three switches she selected. I obediently did as my mother told me, and after I'd broken them from the tree's branch she took them and braided them. After careful inspection, she handed them to me. Then she told me to take them to the fire that was burning in the open hearth in our living room. When I got them to the fire she instructed me to place them in the hot ashes and allow them to roast while she took me over the lesson my teacher had given me.

My mother would carefully and painstakingly read my lesson aloud to me. Then she would have me repeat what she'd read to me without missing a word. This was my mother's routine with each of us in teaching us our lessons; she would model any lesson for each of us, then she'd have us repeat what she'd done for each of us with our lessons. Now, as interesting as it may be, she meted out our punishment for our lack of learning according to our personalities. Only God can make mothers! That is why I'm emphatically convinced that every woman who births a child is not a mother. While my mother was unique and unlike any woman in the community, she clearly had high expectations and a deep, abiding and insatiable thirst for knowledge as it relates to education. Both my parents set high educational goals. There were no exceptions; all of us were required to graduate high school. Beyond completing high school, our efforts of acquiring further education were optional. Of course, attending all church services that were offered by the Baptist denomination was never an option. During my formative years and especially growing up under my parents' domain civility, structure, and an excellent work ethic were not optional. If you lived in the household under their authority, certain behaviors were unspoken regulations that were ingrained in the management and operational procedures of the household. There were never any questions about the hierarchical structure of our household. We, as children, were well cared for and showered frequently with love. As dysfunctional as our home was, we were reared under a heavy hand of authority and love by our parents. We children grew up with a deep and abiding love and respect for God, family, church, school, and community. When I sometimes take a retrospective look back over my life, my memories are overwhelmed by all the love that was bestowed upon me by my parents, church, school, and community. As imperfect as we were as a community—with many deficiencies and tons of deprivation—somehow, we were constantly taught about God's love and the stories from the "book of instruction before leaving the planet Earth"—the Bible. It reinforced and fortified the more positive virtues hidden beneath the outer crusts of the hardships and insurmountable challenges we were confronted with—but at the same time, challenged to overcome.

During our childhood there were difficulties, obstacles, pitfalls, and unforeseeable odds in our pathway; but because we had parents that had a relationship with God by way of fellowship in the church, we were able to rise above and overcome many of the stumbling blocks and negativities in our lives.

More often than I care to mention, there were challenges that I was confronted with; some I overcame, and some stifled me and others impeded and delayed my progress for a while. However, because of God's goodness, power, love, and presence in my life I was determined to keep moving forward. My life story reflects much of what the late great poet Langston Hughes of the Harlem Renaissance depicted in his poem, "Life for me ain't been no crystal stair". More often than I've mentioned in this writing of my life story, Hughes' poem has been a driving force and prime motivator in shaping the tapestry of the formative years in my life. While I give proper and due diligence to my parents, extended family, teachers, and others who built upon the substance and innate qualities of my being, much of these intrinsic qualities had to be molded by external circumstances of the environment in which I grew up.

As I reflect on the past, many things I experienced left me no recourse but to conclude that, had the Lord not been there on my side, where would I be? Many, many times in my life, I have looked at others from my own community who have fallen to negative situations; many succumbed to the detrimental forces that they yielded to, for whatever reasons. Perhaps some of these reasons could be rationalized and some could not. However, that didn't change the tragic outcome of their lives. I am not suggesting that I was insensitive or without compassion to their ultimate state; but I could not allow their disparate lifestyles to directly affect the direction in which my life was going.

I recognize the Creator, God made us, the human race interdependent on each other. Essentially, I am saying the Divine Creator made us to be accountable, respectable, and responsible to each other as far as our abilities and understanding for each other. Nevertheless, we are the net products of our experiences, exposures, and human training. And so within me, I am open to the full expression of God in me. Often times during my childhood growth and development I may have felt lost and alone, believing I was separated from God. Diminished by my sense of limitation and fear, there was time I believed I was not worthy of God's good. Yet as I grew and developed a relationship, I realized my inherent worthiness and that God supplies my every need. The challenges and circumstances of my life may change, but God within is unfailing, steady, and strong.

Through prayer and meditation, I bring awareness to all that I am in God. I begin by focusing on my breath and observing what is happening in my body and emotions. Next, I go deeper into the silence, beyond the physical, and experience the Oneness in Spirit. I then realize I am attuned and aware of the Ultimate Presence. Then and only then, I'm open to the full expression of the God in me.

Over time and much struggle, I realized it was through many trials and tribulations that I began to develop a deeper and abiding relationship with God. The power to change, through a process called disruptive innovation, lies within each of us by choice. This change manifests itself through the way the world thinks and works. It occurs in every aspect of human endeavor and most people can become more creative and innovative—given the right environment and opportunities. I have learned from experience and through an everlasting relationship with God that we develop a deeper understanding of how we can be transformed by faith in Jesus Christ.

As I grow older and more secure in my faith walk, I don't need to mimic the behaviors and customs of this world; I allow God to transform me into a new person by changing the way I think. I'm challenged to give myself fully to God, and it is an ever-evolving process and a concerted effort in my life daily. In a self-centered, greedy, and grasping world, I need to be constantly nurtured and mentored by the Holy Spirit in how to live a Christ-centered, giving life. I realize living in a world of guided missiles and misguided humanity, the world has changed dramatically and is steadily changing rapidly. But I have come to learn and accept that people's longings for love, forgiveness, and the power to change have remained the same. I have come to accept that Jesus Christ, the Great Innovator, continually offers and invites us all to accept, encounter, and experience a new and different life in Him. My constant prayer is, *"Lord, I am thankful for the ways You are changing me. Help me to be open to You and to cooperate with Your work in me. In my daily walk with You, transform me to be like You."*

God takes us as we are, but He never leaves us the way He finds us. My father's mother was a strong influence in my life during my formative years. In fact, I'm told the evening of my birth, my father's mother told my mother, 'there is your teacher and your preacher.' My grandmother was Mrs. Sennie McClellan. She was the mother of three boys and three girls. I am told they hailed from a small town called Helena, Arkansas, and that my family roots can be traced back not only to Africa, but also to the Civil War.

I am told there was a man in our family named General McClellan, and he was responsible for making and supplying saddles to the confederate army. I am told my grandparents' bloodline is not only of African descent, but Indian and Irish as well.

I have fond memories as a boy growing up in Mississippi in that rural community called Long Branch; how my Grandmother Sennie and her sister, Aunt Mary Eliza, used to meet in that old dirt road. As they approached each other they would go through an Indian ritual. My grandmother told me it was an Apache-Choctaw Indian ritual with the broken "spiel chalet" or spoken dialect. Naturally, this was intriguing and mind-boggling to me because I had never seen or heard the likes of this behavior before.

My Grandmother Sennie lived in our home, and so she rendered quite an influence over us children growing up. I was her favorite grandchild; she doted and lavished loads of affection upon me physically and mentally growing up. She was the cook in the big house and my father ran the day-to-day operations of the plantation. My grandmother had a brother who lived in Paxton, Missouri. By profession he was a school master. She frequently told me while I was growing up that I would be a school master just like him!

At a very early age, somehow, I knew I was special. My grandmother used to give me gifts at Christmas. I remember her purchasing me a wagon, tricycle, and many other items, some of which were purchased to mentally stimulate and challenge me as I developed and matured in school. My grandmother used to sit me behind the stove when she cooked in the family home. One of her favorite beverages was Maxwell House coffee. She tried her best to make me like Maxwell House coffee. I just could not like it though; she put too much granulated sugar in it to sweeten it, and therefore I did not like the taste of it. Everything my grandmother had, she always shared it with me. As you may imagine, my grandmother wielded loads of love and influence upon my life, especially during my formative years. My grandmother departed this life December 13, 1954. That was a Monday night. However, the day before she departed she took me out to the clothesline where my mother used to wash the family clothes and hang them on a makeshift clothesline. My mother would clamp them with clothespins to keep them stable to the clothesline. My grandmother gave me a dime wrapped in a black cloth, tied with white thread. She had tied the dime in a special way so that the wrap would make a square. I remember distinctly her words to me were to never rid myself of the dime. I promised her that the dime and me would never part company. When I told my parents, my father took the dime. What I remember most distinctly was the posture that my grandmother held and her stance as she positioned her body before me. Though I was ten years of age, she took careful precautions not to permit me to see her eyes. I have wondered several times since that day why she positioned herself that way. My sanctified imagination has satisfied me with the notion that my grandmother knew the end was imminent; so, in her own protective, loving and caring way, she bid me farewell.

My grandmother taught me values that had a lasting effect and will leave an indelible impression upon my being as long as I live and walk upon these mundane shores called Earth.

She instilled in me how to choose to serve in *being* and in *spirit*. I learned early from her teachings that freedom is a state of being beyond external circumstances; she taught me how to experience freedom regardless of what I see outside of myself and my environment. Early in my life, she taught me how to choose positiveness in my thoughts, feelings, attitudes and perceptions. By choosing to focus and concentrate on the good and not the negative, my spirit would soar and always rise above my external surroundings. For as long as I can remember, she emphasized to me the importance of releasing negative thoughts and emotions and how to feel lighter in mind, body and soul. She also explained to me how to nurture my mind with ideas of health and well-being by staying away from toxic beverages and smoking cigarettes. By doing so, she told me I would experience the freedom of a balanced and productive life. And so, in growing up I developed an outlook in life of positiveness—I expected only good. Ultimately, she taught me freedom is a choice and a state of mind; by holding positive thoughts and feelings, I could experience life to the fullest.

One of the greatest and lasting impressions she left on my life was how to choose to be optimistic in all situations and circumstances; no matter what I am confronted within life, always choose freedom.

My grandmother had three sisters. The youngest sister was called Aunt Eliza-Babe. She had another sister called Aunt Cary Green. I heard her talk of another sister she fondly called Aunt Dove. I also heard her speak of another sister called Aunt Hattie. These sisters had their own families too. My grandmother's family consisted of three boys and three girls. Aunt Beulah was the oldest girl, followed by Aunt Lurlean and Aunt Bertha; each of my aunts had their own families. My grandmother's oldest son was named Clarence, my father Albert Lee was the second son, and Phillip McClellan was the youngest. Of all Grandmother Sennie's sons, my father Rev. Albert L. McClellan was the preacher in the family.

I am told my Uncle Clarence lived a very interesting and intriguing life. I do know he was once married to a lady, Aunt Minnie, and they had two children, namely Clarence, Jr. and Lurlean. I'm also told Uncle Clarence had other children, a son named John L McClellan, and another son who was fondly called by his pen name, 'Gippy'. My father's youngest brother was never married; I'm told he lived the life of a gigolo and a pimp, and that he died in infamy at the age of thirty-two, having contracted syphilis.

I now bring my mother to the forefront of my discussion of my immediate family's genealogy. I am told my mother's family came from a small and rural community called Hoffman, a little village located near Belmont M.B. Church; just north of Durant, and just east of a community called Second Pilgrim Rest. My mother's father lived on a parcel of land with a long hill called the Pempleton's Hill. My mother said that her mother's genealogy is of the Montgomery family line, and that her father came from the genealogy of the Pempletons. My mother's father had a number of brothers, as well as a sister whose name was Mariah. As I think about my Aunt Mariah, I have fond memories of this lady who wielded quite an influence in my life.

Aunt Mariah had one daughter whose pen name was 'Coop'. She was married to a man named Willie Hawkins. They had a number of children. My mother's Aunt Mariah was quite an independent religious matriarch. There were times my mother allowed Aunt Mariah to come and stay with us. As spiritual and religious as she was, she had a very humorous and devious human side. Aunt Mariah lived to be well up in age before she transitioned this life. I am sure what I most remember about her was the wisdom and the predictions she spoke over our lives as children. While we toiled in the scorching-hot summer's sun picking cotton and gathering different produce Aunt Mariah would be right in the midst of us with her long cotton sack, picking cotton or whatever else we were doing on our farm. While she brought a sense of warmth, connection, and a spirit of solidarity to the family, her genuine love for our well-being and family unity shined as a bright beacon of light over us. She was high-spirited, spiritual and well-connected to God through relationship, fellowship, and friendship. As I reflect on my mother's family members, they were peace-loving, cohesive, and tenacious as it relates to hard work. They were people who believed in owning whatever they worked for. Frankly, they were people that did not mind hard work as long as the goal was ownership.

It must have been shortly after 1944 when my mother and father and the family moved from the Edsville Plantation Village community where I was born. We moved about two miles to another part of the same farming plantation community called Long Branch. The same family owned this community. It was just another part of the same plantation belonging to the brother of Master D'Mathis. This brother had been cohabitating with one of my great aunt's daughters. I'm told he had once lived in the house we moved to after we left Edsville. This house was a fine elaborate spacious home. It was well-constructed, and it had an adjoining well called a cistern. This house and over one hundred acres of land was given to my family by way of a verbal contract, due to a promise made to my Grandmother Sennie because the master's brother had killed her niece. I am told the death occurred because she violated the established code of conduct. The 'code' was that whenever a white man, especially in the south, cohabitated with a Black woman in his home, it was an established yet unwritten rule: whenever she came to his home, always come to the back door for entrance. On this particular Saturday night-Sunday morning when she came to see her master for cohabitating purposes, she took it upon herself to knock on the front door instead of going to the back door. It was her last knock upon any earthly door; as she knocked upon his door she was answered with the blast of a gun. Some family members said he used a pistol, others said he used a shotgun. Regardless of the type or kind of gun he used, his aim was accurate, and the shot took my cousin's life upon impact. The evidence showed, without question and beyond speculation, who the perpetrator was and the victim as well. Upon the commission of such a heinous and despicable crime, white men do what white men do, with respect to offering restitution for such a dastardly deed. The plantation master's family told my Grandmother Sennie [who was the cook in the big house where the masters lived] that the house where her niece was killed, and the surrounding land would be a 'gift' to her and her family. Well, I want you to know my mother did not believe or settle for that blatant and bold lie. Now this was the premise and promise which my family had acknowledged to move in the house; but my mother never believed for one minute that the master's family was truthful with their promises.

The family was almost complete with the birth of the children when we moved. In 1946, my youngest brother was born in the 'white house' and with his birth, that completed our family. At best, we had been living there about five years. My mother, the conscientious, frugal, and resourceful woman that she was, always preserved and stored not only the resources on the farm, but her money as well.

My mother was a woman with an indomitable, tenacious, clever, and persistent personality. My mother's parents were Mr. Richard and Mrs. Causie Montgomery Pempleton. My mother was born December 24, 1902. She died March 8, 1984. My mother was the oldest girl of seven children; five boys and two girls. She and her siblings were born on a farm five miles north of Durant, Mississippi. The farm had a long hill about a quarter of a mile in length, called the Pempleton's Hill. The family's church was the Belmont Missionary Baptist Church, which is still in existence today. My mother's and father's first schools were the Grant School; Huckleberry School; Liberty Hill School; and the Rosenwald School. My mother completed elementary and junior high school at the aforementioned schools. After obtaining her junior high school education, she journeyed on to Holmes County Training School. There she met our father, the late Rev. Albert L. McClellan; they were classmates. She completed the first semester of high school, which means she had one semester to complete before graduation. The second semester, my father asked our mother's parents for her hand in marriage. I was told my mother's father objected vehemently. Grandma Causie responded by saying to Grandpa Richard, "let Jannie and 'Jake" get married. You and I married, didn't we, Richard?"

I later learned mother went to great lengths to let everyone know that she was not pregnant. She and Daddy were in love, and in those days getting married was the appropriate thing to do when the love bug 'bit' real hard. What a lesson for today's generation, huh? At any rate, their firstborn was a girl, born one year following their marriage. As perhaps has already been mentioned, my mother was a very resourceful, entrepreneurial, and enterprising woman by nature. She was very loving, compassionate, empathizing, and understanding with respect to her children. She was a very God-fearing mother; yet she was demanding, commanding, gentle, and fun-loving at times. She had an extraordinary sense of humor. Truly, without a doubt, she was a very 'rare gem'. I have yet to encounter, see, or hear a woman who was as dedicated to the advancement, improvement, and progress of her husband and children as my mother. Frankly, she was the epitome of virtue, justice, and fair play in life. I saw in her Micah 6:8 *"He has shown you, O mortal, what is good. And what does the Lord require of you? To act justly and to love mercy and to walk humbly with your God."*. I saw this verse come to fulfillment in her lifetime, demonstrated and illustrated in her mannerisms and lifestyle. I saw her live out an active definition of virtue; which is the 'trade unionism of traditional marriage'.

Above all the qualities she possessed as a person, she was fallible, and she possessed all the frailties that accompany the human experience. However, her character was impeccable, her virtues were noble, and her spiritual insights were as keen as a razor's edge.

She was fierce and courageous as an eagle when it came to her household and its affairs. She was relentless in her savvy, she was indomitable in spirit with respect to inspiration and motivation, and gentle in guiding her children in the understanding of wisdom, knowledge, and the practical matters of life. She was flexible and agile in the midst of the storms that frequently challenged her in the ups and downs of everyday life. Frequently, she put every effort she could possibly summon in attempting to answer all my questions about life at a very early age. God knows, I had many! For those questions she couldn't answer about any-and-all matters of life, she had an uncanny and simplistic way of allaying my fears and consoling my wandering mind. But most of all, she was good at calming, soothing, and giving me the 'blessed assurance' through Jesus. She let me know that in time it would become clearer in understanding, if only I would get to know God through relationship, fellowship, and friendship by trusting and obeying.

Finally, my mother instilled in me a work ethic par excellence that is second to none. As I'd go about my daily occupations I remember hearing her say, "if a job you've once begun, never leave it until it is done. Be its labor great or small, do it well or not at all!" Personally, I don't know anyone on the planet who could've been my mother, except Mrs. Jannie Pempleton McClellan.

CHAPTER TWO

As I write this book, my father has been deceased for thirty-eight years and my mother has been deceased for thirty-one years. Among the ten siblings to reach adulthood, my brother, William McClellan was the first to transition this life. William 'Joe" McClellan transitioned in December, 2011. The second sibling to pass away was my oldest sister. She made her transition March 8, 2012 at about 9:50p.m. in Chicago, Illinois. The third sibling to transition this life was my oldest living brother, who was a fraternal twin. His name was Eddie B. McClellan. He passed away on February 21, 2015. He was a patient in the Midway Renaissance Nursing Home in Chicago, Illinois. As I continued to write this book, seven of us are still living.

Ms. Lyneva Gipson, my sister, is a resident of Detroit, Michigan. She has two daughters, Mrs. Karen Daniels and Mrs. Jacquelyn Blanding and their families. My sister, Mrs. Nannie C. Fitzgerald, is the late Eddie B. McClellan's fraternal twin. She now resides in Fort Worth, Texas with her daughter, Dr. Lynette Alexis and family. My sister, Mrs. Causie Cobbs, resides in Chicago, Illinois with her son Derrick Cobbs, his wife, Vanessa, and their family. Causie also has daughters that reside in Atlanta, Georgia with their families. My sister and her husband, Mrs. Ora and Mr. James Cain, reside in Durant, Mississippi and have two sons; Dr. Jarrett Cain, who practices medicine at Penn State University and Mr. Cedric Cain, a licensed certified school teacher. My youngest sister, Ms. Lena McClellan resides in New Orleans, Louisiana. She is a retired public school teacher of New Orleans, Louisiana. She has two sons, Charles McClellan of Atlanta, Georgia, and Carl Strange of New York. Charles and his daughter Gionni McClellan are residents of Atlanta, Georgia. Mr. Albert L. McClellan is the baby of the family. Currently, he is a resident of Chicago, Illinois. He is a Vietnam veteran, and is the father of three children, Albert L. McClellan, II; Kimitrea McClellan; and K'Shana McClellan. I'm the oldest living sibling and son of my parents. I'm the father of two children. My daughter is Terri Lynn McClellan, who is a resident of Milwaukee, Wisconsin and my son Kelly is a resident of Chicago, Illinois. Joann and I have been married thirty-eight years. We have no children; of course, we have "Paco", our family pooch! Paco is a pedigreed Shih Tzu by breed. We are told nobody knows how the ancient breeders managed to mix together "a dash of lion; several teaspoons of rabbit; a couple of ounces of domestic cat; one part court jester, and dash of ballerina; a pinch of old man, a bit of beggar, a tablespoon of monkey; one part baby seal, a dash of teddy bear—and for the rest, dog of Tibetan and Chinese origin. What a colorful description!

The Shih Tzu [pronounced 'sheed-zoo', 'shid-zoo', or 'sheet-sue'] is a small, regal dog with long, pretty, abundant locks, and a distinctive face that melts many hearts upon observation. They are naturally intelligent and have a very friendly attitude. The breed can boast of a classy background. They were originally kept by royal Chinese families during the Ming Dynasty. With their flowing hair sweeping the ground and their topknot elegantly tied, this breed might appear snobbish and sophisticated, suited only for lying about a palace on silk pillows. Nothing could be further from the truth, however; Shih Tzus are beautiful, friendly, lively, independent, and devoted companions. The Shih Tzu is enormously appealing, very loyal; even onlookers and grudging dog observers find it hard to resist this breed. The Shih Tzu simply doesn't allow anyone to ignore him or her. They were bred to be friendly companions. They don't hunt, herd, or guard; and these qualities make them distinct and different from all other breeds. They love nothing more than to meet, greet, and entertain friends and strangers. Just know Shih Tzus make friends wherever they go. Not only is this member of the toy group good-natured, independent, intelligent, and friendly; they are highly adaptable. They are as well-suited to apartments and homes in the city as to life on a country farm. They love children and they tolerate other animals. Although, our Shih Tzu is a sturdy dog, his small size puts him at a disadvantage. We are always mindful to supervise his interactions with children to prevent him from accidentally hurting himself from rough play. Finally, interestingly, we found out that this breed is sometimes called the "chrysanthemum dog", a nickname that describes the way the hair on his face grows out in all directions. He looks like a flower with a nose for a center. Our boy Paco, the joy of our family: there is never a dull moment in his presence. He is very territorial by nature and habit. He loves Joann, and he also loves to be pampered, bathed, and entertained by my wife's many different antics with him. The little fellow has his own warehouse of toys. He selects and plays with them at his own convenience. I can honestly say Paco is a bonafide member of the family. He never ceases to amaze me with his playful antics. I often take him with me to grab food, to the post office, clothes cleaners, and different stores when I need to pick up a few odds and ends needed in our home. Many times as we're riding in the car, he will almost go into a trance while expressing his feelings to me just by constantly staring at me. As we continue on our way, either going to the store or returning from an errand, he will come from the passenger's side of the car and climb into my lap. Paco has so many ways he communicates with the both of us. He clearly knows the difference between JoJo and me—and I am convinced he tolerates me, but he loves JoJo. He spends most of his time in JoJo's part of the house.

Another amazing thing I have observed about our little pooch: he has to have a master. Sometimes he and I will sit on the sofa together, either watching a particular television show, or a football game, or several different football games. He'll climb in my lap, grab my finger, and start to bite down on it gently until I raise my voice; then he'll release the grip on my finger. When he initially started this behavior, I didn't pay too much attention to it. But as time progressed and I noticed the frequency of him displaying this behavior with me, it finally registered in my psyche that this was his way of expressing his need to have a master.

Paco never ceases to amaze us. He has an amazing sense of humor, and yet he is unique in the many other intelligent qualities he possesses. I have yet to experience another dog so smart in so many ways. His emotions run the full spectrum of behaviors common with his pedigree. In another world, Paco had to be a superior being, in charge of a lot of other inferior beings. Paco has taught the both of us so much.

I have talked extensively about my childhood, my parents, and my extended family. At this juncture, I will conclude this section talking about my immediate family and my accomplishments, vocation, and avocation.

1957 was a very important transitional period in my life. I grew up in the Long Branch community, and as a result, that was the extent of my familiarity with the outside world. However, because of the gallant and extraordinary efforts of the African American lawyer Thurgood Marshall and his team of lawyers in the winning of the Brown vs. the Board of Public Education case, the lives of African Americans changed from a rural experience to an urban encounter throughout the continental United States of America. Brown vs. the Board of Public Education dealt primarily with the integration of the school system in the United States of America. Because of the victory in that landmark case, I am a living benefactor of its actions and my life changed forever. So did the lives of many African Americans, not only in the state of Mississippi, but across the breadth and width of this country.

For the very first time, integration was experienced and shared among ourselves in a collective way. Prior to the victory of this case, African Americans were restricted and contained in local hamlets, and isolated—connected only by the many pastors and preachers in the Black churches in America. The future of many Black children was changed because of this case won by the late Thurgood Marshall and his team of lawyers in 1954.

Many grade schools in the South had been held in local churches, homes, and hamlets where Black people were densely populated; school integration provided the opportunity to be transported to the schools in major cities in those states. In my case, it was Holmes County Training School in the city of Durant, Mississippi.

I was in seventh grade when I experienced my first big yellow bus ride from the Long Branch Elementary to Holmes County Training School in Durant, Mississippi. I was behind in my proper grade when I entered middle school; but let me quickly say it wasn't because of ignorance, it was because of deprivation. Wherever there is a community of people there will be cliques and caste systems of categorizing people if for no other reason than their material or family status. I am sure I was retained by the teacher not because I was ignorant; but because of a punitive and subjective reason that had nothing to do with academics. I recall vividly after having entered Holmes County Training School, the principal recognized my ability and aptitude and moved immediately to advance me and put me in my correct grade. His wife prevented it with prejudice. The principal's wife was very flamboyant, vocal and dramatic. She was a very enigmatic and unique person, and she was the dominant force in managing and operating the school.

Back in the day, Holmes County Training School had its own distinctive personality. We were surrounded by other neighboring schools; we had several schools that fed into Holmes County Training and gave it such a distinctive personality. Our mascot was the "Yellow Jackets". We were a part of the Southwestern Athletic Conference, and we moved into the new school in September 1960.

Our class was the first class to graduate from the new school: Durant Attendance Center. The interesting and fascinating part of the entire experience was that an entire new world was opening up to me. Experiencing urban life was the first time my world expanded beyond the cotton and cornfields of my immediate community.

As you might imagine, there was no more getting up at five o'clock in the morning dealing with a multitude of chores at home, then walking about a mile to school. After having gotten there—especially the boys—our job was getting brush and wood from the wooded area around the school to keep the fire burning in the pot-belly heater that sat in the middle of the old "shotgun" building, which kept us warm in the wintertime. How well do I remember the solid "shotgun" structure. It had a midsection in the center of the building that was sometimes a makeshift curtain or a partially-built wooded partition—whatever the teachers deemed necessary to adequately separate the elementary students from the middle school students.

Entering the seventh grade, I thought, 'Holmes County Training School, here I come!' I was straight out of the rural area-country, for the lack of a better expression. I was meeting new people; riding on a big yellow school bus; meeting and getting acquainted with new students from the surrounding communities, hamlets, villages and clans I never knew existed. It was astonishing, amazing. Some people were young adults in the seventh grade; that was amazing to me! Then there were students significantly younger than I was in the seventh grade. There were those who had gotten caught up by the system and circumstances beyond their control, and as a result had become victimized by extenuating conditions beyond their control. However, be that as it was, time and fate kept on moving.

Arriving in Durant, Mississippi at Holmes County Training School ushered in favorable and unfavorable circumstances. Our seventh-grade class was so large we had to be put into the auditorium. Our first teacher was a man named Julius Buchannon. There must have been about seventy-five or eighty of us in the class. Above and beyond that huge number, we were a contained group. Mr. Julius Buchannon taught us several different subjects, such as: Geography, American Citizenship, English, Science, and Mathematics. Fortunately, the next year the new school, Durant Attendance Center, was completed. When we entered D.A.C., we were eighth graders.

We were then separated into sections. That was the first time in my junior high school experience we were separated into sections, and we also had to exchange classroom every hour for at least five to six periods a day. During that experience, different teachers taught you different subjects. I recall distinctly, I had this one teacher who taught me Geometry and Mississippi History. Her name was Ms. Ann Gates. I'm sure the things that impressed me most about Ms. Gates was her knowledge of her subject matter and how she taught me. She was impeccably neat, she was a very graceful woman and she also had a gentle, yet firm demeanor. I had other teachers as well; but as you know, as you move through your elementary, middle school, and high school years, some teachers impact your learning experience more than others. Frankly, it is the same way with your classmates. My classmates that left an indelible impression on my learning experience during my high school years were Mary Ellen Hunter; Shirley Winters; Geneva Edwards; Patricia Gordon; Mattie Pearl Seawood; Alonzo Brown; Johnny Wilbur [Cake]; James Stringley [Hamp]; James Seawood; John Boyette; and Ann Gallain.

Then of course, I also had high school instructors that left impactful experiences on my life; one such instructor was Mr. Williams, who taught me 9th grade Science during my freshman year of high school at Durant Attendance Center. He left such an indelible impression on my life during my high school career that, until this day, I recall the way he taught me Biology. He taught with a passion and an inspiration that lit a fire in my spirit.

He left D.A.C. and went to California. The last I heard of him, he had gone into medicine. I was not at all amazed or surprised when the news was told to me. Another teacher that touched me deeply in high school was Ms. Adele Whitaker. She taught me 10th grade Algebra. She also taught with a passion and a special inspiration. She was a native of Meridian, Mississippi. I don't know what college or university she attended; nor do I know what college or university Mr. Williams attended. Mrs. Poindexter was another memorable teacher who taught me high school English. She was a graduate of Mississippi Valley State University. I remember Mr. Sullivan teaching me World History; in my opinion, he was a much better instructor than his wife. I say that because his approach to teaching was much more of a consummate approach. He taught from a holistic perspective, meaning he was much more sensitive to the total condition of the student's condition than his wife. Mr. J.L. Sullivan was a consummate educator in his approach to the student's overall dilemma. He always made a conscious effort to identify with the condition of a student, whatever the circumstances may have been. Then he would gently and patiently correct, prod, and compel the student into the learning situation. Many times, even the student was unaware of the gentle correction in this approach and technique he frequently employed in his teaching.

Now, his wife's approach was altogether different. Mrs. Sullivan taught World Literature. She had a variety of approaches in her arsenal to get her point across in teaching a student. I suspect being the lady that she was, she had a plethora of tricks she employed in getting a student's attention. First of all, Mrs. Sullivan made it her business to

54

know the family histories of her students. Once those facts were established, they were among several other variables she had utilized in her methodology and technique of teaching. When she'd completed her background analysis of each student, you could rest assured she had a pretty accurate profile of what a student's potential was within a week of being enrolled in her class. Her nickname was 'Chief', because someone affectionately decided one day that's who she should be! Unlike her husband the principal, there was always an unforeseen method to her approach. She was wise enough to know the more background information she had on a student prior to teaching them, the better chance she could determine their success in achieving in an advanced environment. Why? Because she would have done a verbal assessment of the student's family tree. Because of this approach, among other things in her bag of tricks for teaching, she kept the standard high for student enrollment at Durant Attendance Center. It was a known, universal, and non-negotiable fact: not just anyone could enroll and graduate from D.A.C. Consequently, Mr. and Mrs. Sullivan kept the academic standards high as long as they were in the forefront at D.A.C. In years following their tenure, the standards were significantly compromised to coincide with the national norms that have attacked public education and the public-school system in this nation.

As you well know, during our generation America was challenged to make a thorough examination of herself on a multitude of fronts regarding her attitude and behavior towards minorities in this country. As a result of the many challenges that were brought before her, public education was one area where able and qualified African Americans could assist in lifting the iron shoe of segregation and oppression off their own necks in a major and significant way through the courts, political and educational systems in this country. I acknowledge and express my gratitude and appreciation to the many—regardless of race, creed, or ethnicity—that were there in the forefront of the struggle, who made it possible for me to have been the benefactor of a quality education.

I am certain that I speak for many in my biological family, my community, and my generation, who have high praise and gratitude to those who made it all possible. Let me say, incidentally, I have classmates who graduated from Durant Attendance Center who did not go on to institutions of higher learning as I did. However, it does not mean that they could have been any less successful than I have been—quite the contrary, as I review them in the corners and imaginary section of my mind. Some are yet here and some have made their transitions. At the end of the day, all are governed by the hand that fate dealt us in the game of life. Some of us did what we could, given the circumstances and conditions that confronted us. And as I move on to close this chapter of my life, there are many things I chose not to put to print in my book. However, I will admit my high school career was very tumultuous, fraught with challenges, and confronted with decisions I made. And yet, because of the parental guidance and a loving mother, better decisions were made for me.

CHAPTER THREE

Because of my mother's tender touch, uncompromising persistence, and unconditional love I was catapulted into a college career like siblings before me.

Unconventional circumstances coupled with a strong and swift hand convinced me to just participate, and not ask any questions. Being caught up in a situation of my own immature choosing—and yet considering the options before me—my only priority was to yield to my mother's command or go down the path my immature and irrational thinking had driven me into.

My father was nowhere to be seen; but be most assured: his presence and influence counted heavily on the final outcome of my decision. My mother and father operated with those dynamics in rearing and training their children. Well, as fate would dictate the rules of my decision, I really didn't have any bargaining chips in the decision process anyway. Realistically, I was their son and yes, I had graduated high school. But beyond that, I had no input that was influential or could make a tangible difference in the outcome of my fate. My Dad had dictated the rules to my mother as to what the final decision was, commensurate to the rule I had broken in our home regarding his property—namely, his automobile. So there I was, standing before the judge and jury; my freedom or incarceration was in my mother's hands. Now, let me just say my father pastored four of the churches in the neighboring communities. He was well-respected in the community in which we lived by all people, the dominant culture notwithstanding. Here I was, fortunate enough to have graduated high school, but could not act right with my father's car on the night of the Junior/Senior High School Prom.

My father had an impeccable reputation among all people. The Caucasian man who had rendered his wrecker service had charged $20; I did not have that. The Gulf service station owner [also white] who had put the disconnected muffler back on my father's car had charged $5; I didn't have that either! And so as you can imagine, everything that had been done to my father's car had been done *on credit,* and at the expense of his stellar reputation. One of the incredible and fascinating things about youth is that great rush of natural hormones that flood the male anatomy. Consequently, if he is not surrounding by a praying family, extending family, and a good praying spiritual community, there is no way he can transcend the snares, traps and many obstacles that plague the journey of the African American male. I know, even with a strong nuclear family and God-fearing parents that were among the few property owners in the Long Branch community, the statistics were thin; the state's Bureau of Census was replete with African American males of my generation then and now, who were not supposed to have survived. But there is God, who created the universe in its entirety and holds all animate and inanimate objects in sync. His Divine Providence and Plan has ordered my steps from my conception in my mother's womb, even until the present.

I had disobeyed my father and wrecked the family car by consuming too much corn whiskey and Thunderbird wine on the night of the Junior/Senior Prom. In my foolish, immature, and inexperienced thinking, I thought by me working for a Caucasian named Mr. Westman, that I could go to him and borrow thirty dollars to pay the existing debts that I had created by wrecking my father's car. My job was baling hay that is gathered and harvested during the spring and summer to feed the livestock during the winter months, and my wage was a meager four dollars for an eight-hour day's work. But you know, on the journey call life, I've experienced the rude awakening that life itself is a school. And on the journey of life, there are no rehearsals! I have further concluded: all that does not kill you on this journey will pulverize or soften you in life's preparation. Another conclusion I have reached is that our experiences in life will either bring us closer to God or drive us further away from Him. Lastly, God has a purpose for each member in a family's life.

While a nuclear family consisting of both a mother and father may have any number of children, the mother knows the strengths and weaknesses of each child in that nuclear family. Now, my mother knew I was the son that learned *best* and *most* from my experiences in life; and so she allowed me to make my mistakes in my life during my formative years. However, I was always assured of her unconditional and sacrificial love and faithfulness. When I went to Mr. Westman for the thirty-dollar loan, his refusal was devastating to me, for any number of reasons. For one, I knew I was a young man and I knew I was an honest man; even back then, if I made you a promise, you could be most assured I'd see it through. Finally, I was in a situation where only Mr. Westman or my parents could have rescued me from the perils of the dominant culture's system. When Mr. Westman refused to extend me the loan, my alternative was the County Penitentiary.

You must remember: all I had given to the other two Caucasian men were promises. The one who had pulled my father's car out of the ditch and announced the cost of $20 had said to me, "if you don't have my $20 by 8:00p.m. this Saturday evening, I can assure you the County Penitentiary is where you are going!" Now, the man I owed the $20 was a bit more civil and compassionate, because he knew my father well, and he also knew my father was a pillar and a man of great influence in the community. He also knew my father was a minister and he pastored four Baptist churches in the Afro-American community in four different adjacent communities connected to the city of Durant. This man knew my father's temperament, and he also knew that my father stood at the head of his family. He further knew and respected my father's directive about the behavior and disposition of his children, especially his boys. After a swift and stern warning from him about my father's car, he moved quickly to make the necessary repairs and he washed my father's car. Upon my departure from his business establishment, I headed home to my father with his car. After encountering him and attempting to explain my behavior, he approached me with haste and started hitting me with a newspaper, at which time I headed for higher ground! I ran to the pasture and the woods; my mother took matters into her hands following that encounter.

She and my father had a heated conversation about my future, and for that matter, my living condition. His directive was for me to get out of his house, because I had a younger brother; he felt drastic and punitive measures needed to be my punishment, because lesser measures would send the wrong message to my younger brother. So, that put the final consequence for my behavior in my mother's court. After exhausting every means I knew to get the twenty-five dollars to pay the debt I owed for service rendered on credit, my mother got the money from somewhere. That Saturday evening about 8:00p.m., I was fortunate enough to catch a ride to Durant with a distant cousin to go and pay my debts. Now, after paying my debts was when I was shocked into the rude reality of who my friends were in Durant. You know, I'd had the uncanny and naive experience of believing I had a lot of male friends in Durant! However, when I messed up my father's car and embarrassed my family's name at my senior high school prom, I began to learn and understand what my father and a few others had been attempting to tell me all along.

The fallacies and euphoric feelings of youth have a way of navigating us through an unrealistic path of life until we find out better. As I write this book, and as I think about it retrospectively, I am not so sure that it's a bad thing to be ignorant and naïve. I have lived long enough to find out that ignorance is a state of unconsciousness that, through self-refinement, will be quickly remedied. By the same token, if you don't permit yourself to learn as you encounter the different phases of life, there is no growth and refinement.

But little did I know, there is someone always standing and observing as we go through the different phases of our teenage years. There was a young beautiful woman whom I was totally unaware had been observing me and was quite attracted to me. When my boys acted as if I had committed an unpardonable sin by messing up during prom night, this beautiful princess, one of Durant's finest and most attractive females, invited me over to her place for a candlelit evening for two, with the appropriate alcoholic beverage. During that encounter I was carefully, patiently, and lovingly given the assurance that indeed, I had not done any more than any other curious, maturing and intelligent young man would do, given my age, ability and temperament.

As the evening progressed I was enchanted, mesmerized, and engaged in moments and hours of ecstasy in the basics of how a woman should be loved. We also experienced intellectual, mental and emotional stimulation. Out of that encounter came a long and enduring relationship that lasted the duration of my college career, and even beyond the days that I spent in institutions of higher learning. The woman not only gave me my first encounter with a real woman, she also taught me the fundamentals of how a woman should be loved and handled. It was a traumatic and rude episode I had encountered as a high school graduate; however, as fate would have it, the experience landed me in the arms and embrace of a willing and beautiful woman who not only possessed all the femininity any young man of my age and caliber would desire; but also the intellect, wisdom, compassion and temperament necessary to move me and equip me for the next very important phase of my life.

Can you imagine a young, country high school graduate making a nuisance of himself at the high school prom? And subsequent to the experience, thinking the whole world was his enemy. But as fate would have it, he stepped into the arms of a beautiful woman who picked him up, dusted him off, and reassured him that he hadn't done any more than any other young man would have done, considering his age, experience, background, and familiarity with the world at large.

When our encounter was over, I walked away from the experience a much more self-assured young man, knowing I had not done anymore than a young man would have done, given my circumstances. The woman and I became lasting friends even beyond the boundaries of our planet experience. So, away I went to Clarksdale, Mississippi in May, 1964. A young man with the initials M.C. and I left Durant during the summer of 1964. Off we went to the delta part of the state of Mississippi to one of its major cities located in the northeastern part of the state. Clarksdale is southwest of Memphis, Tennessee, and it is one of Mississippi's major cities, situated in the county of Coahoma. The junior college my friend and I journeyed to was Coahoma Junior College.

When we arrived in Clarksdale in May, 1964 it was the first time in our lives either of us had ever left Durant to be on our own. My mother and father took me to the Trailways Bus Station in Durant. There I met my friend and classmate, M.C. My mother had fixed my favorite meal, which was fried chicken and coconut cake. At that particular time, the Trailways bus line was confined to the hills of Mississippi, while the Greyhound bus line was confined to the Delta portion of the state. My parents had carefully and consciously seen to it that we were situated and comfortably boarded on the Trailways bus.

CHAPTER FOUR

Back then, leaving home was like leaving the community. Our church had prayed for me, and certain members had given me words of wisdom, along with their do's and don'ts. Notwithstanding, these words of wisdom were in conjunction with the words of wisdom our parents had already given us. When we left home our parents, church, school, and the community sent us off. They had no problem in letting us know that *we* were representing all of *them*. We were admonished to study hard, be obedient to our instructors, and don't forget the church. In other words, don't forget the way we had been taught and raised; no matter who you met and interacted with, always stay grounded and rooted in your family's values, home training, church, and community values. They also taught us to gravitate towards and try to seek out people that had values similar to our own. I recall vividly when we met other students from the surrounding villages, neighborhoods, and communities we would try to claim the major city closest to where we were born and reared.

Back in the day, we really had to be integrated among ourselves before we were exposed and inculcated into the dominant and wider culture. It's funny how I used to observe and watch the struggles and efforts of many of my school mates. Some were classmates that were never able to assimilate and integrate themselves into the collegiate atmosphere. So many of them just quit and many others, for whatever reasons, were not able to make the adjustments or adapt to collegiate life.

Back in the day, the Greyhound bus lines were in the Mississippi Delta and the Trailways bus lines were in the hills of Mississippi, so where you lived in the state dictated which bus you caught and how far you could travel before making your connection to Greyhound or Trailways. In the case of my friend and myself, after graduating high school and leaving Durant to get to Clarksdale, we had to get Trailways to Winona, Mississippi, and change to catch another Trailways bus to Tchula, Mississippi. The third bus was Greyhound, that took us straight into Clarksdale. Of course, that was our destination for Coahoma Junior College. My friend and I arrived in Clarksdale on a Saturday evening. We must have arrived in Clarksdale at about 5:00pm. Now mind you, Coahoma Junior and Aggie High School were situated on the same campus. Coahoma Junior College and Aggie High School were exactly 7 miles from the city of Clarksdale. When we arrived in Clarksdale you could get a taxi cab to take you to the campus for a dollar, or you could catch a ride the 'hobo' way: by using a method called 'thumbing'. Since it was our first time away from home, we decided to get a taxi to take us to the campus.

The campus was located near a city called Friar Point. This little township was more like a village, a place that had a cotton gin and perhaps a United States Post Office. The major staple crops in Mississippi during the days I attended Coahoma Jr. College were cotton and corn. Most of my classmates were from agrarian communities; many of us were from meager and humble beginnings. One of the major motivators for us attending college was to get away from the physicality and routines of the agriculture life, which many of us were accustomed to.

I would not hesitate to say that, in the history of this country, these were the worst of times and yet the best of times for African Americans. It was during this era that America was challenged to have an honest assessment and thorough analysis of herself as far as race relations were concerned. Not only that, she was challenged to review her policies educationally and economically. America was challenged to extend and make opportunities available to the African American community.

Organizations such as the Rockefeller and the Rhodes foundations and several other philanthropic and charitable organizations assisted African Americans in getting out of poverty. And so, it was no accident that avenues were open for many of us to better ourselves through education. Some of us recognized these opportunities, and many of us did not. I could guess there were numerous reasons why many of us did not seize the opportunity; but to do so would be sheer speculation. That said, these were the best times in the era of the oppression of us as a people to take advantage of the opportunities extended by private organizations as well as the government.

After getting to the campus we were told our living quarters were the athletic dormitory. We met Mr. Green, who was the head coach of the football players. He was also the director of the athletic dormitory. After meeting Mr. Green, he gave us a brief tour of our living quarters. He also took us to the cafeteria that Monday morning. We were introduced to the kitchen and cafeteria staff. We were also told we would receive two meals per day, Monday through Friday.

Ms. Moore was the chief dietician. She was very friendly and cordial. She gave us the schedule when the cafeteria would be available. We were served breakfast and lunch Monday through Friday. We quickly got the schedule for the cafeteria committed to memory. Dean Wheatley and his family lived in the quarters provided for the students' dormitory.

Dean Wheatley and I became fond of each other shortly after our introduction. He also taught Social Studies for the college. Shortly after our acquaintance, he approached me to babysit for his family. Of course, I quickly agreed and that was my first job. Mr. and Mrs. Wheatley had a little boy and a little girl; to the best of my memory they could not have been more than a year apart in age. They were very charming and sweet little children. They were well-behaved, and Mrs. Wheatley kept them very clean and well-nurtured.

When my friend and I first arrived at the college, naturally we were in awe. The first person we met was Mr. Johnson, the janitor for the high school and junior college. Mr.

Johnson's nickname was "Prof", short for professor. Mr. McQuien was the principal of Aggie High School, and Dr. B.F. McLaurin was the President of Coahoma Junior College. Coahoma Jr. College was a direct extension of Jackson State College at the time. In other words, one could enroll to attend Coahoma Jr. College, graduate, and go to Jackson State College or Jackson State University without losing academic credits, because Jackson State College's and Jackson State University's academic curriculums were compatible with Coahoma Jr. College's academic curriculum. They both had credit hours set up on a quarterly basis rather than as semesters; when a student transferred to Jackson State University from Coahoma Jr. College, there was no loss of any academic credit hours. However, that was not the case if a student transferred to Alcorn State University or Mississippi Valley State University, because these universities were set up on a semesters basis.

Coahoma Jr. College was a feeder school for Jackson State College/University. That is precisely why when most students graduated from Coahoma Jr. College, they matriculated at Jackson State College/University.

Now, when my friend and I got up that first Monday morning and followed Mr. Johnson's instruction he saw that we were nervous, and he also saw that we were not familiar with Clarksdale. After we had introduced ourselves, the next appropriate thing to do was state why we were there and explain why we had arrived at the beginning of summer, rather than fall. Normally we would have been there in September; but we told him we had arrived for the summer. We had just graduated high school and had heard about Coahoma Jr. College; we had arrived early because we were interested in work. He then told us about Mrs. Whiteside, the dean of the college. Of course, I did most of the talking, my friend M.C. did most of the listening.

Mr. Johnson pointed out the college's administration building to us and instructed us that we were to get to the building between 10am and 11am. He emphasized that this was the usual time Mrs. Whiteside entered the administration building. We followed his instruction precisely and sure enough, Mrs. Whiteside came strolling down the long hallway with that stern but welcoming look on her face. The negotiation starting between my friend and me as to which one of us was going to approach her. With all things considered and given my circumstance at the time, I really did not consider that task a challenge. I approached her with trepidation and caution, with as much respect and humility as one could muster, knowing her status and position at the college. After calling her name three times, I am certain she heard me; but you know back then, adults were led by and operated with the Holy Spirit. In other words, the frequency and the rapidity of my calling her name somehow communicated a note of seriousness and anxiousness concerning why I wanted her attention. She stopped and turned around with grace, mercy and compassion, and said "yes, can I help you young men?"

"Yes ma'am!," I replied. "We came from Durant, Mississippi to go to school. We don't have money. We were wondering if we could find work to pay for our attending school. We are willing to work in any area or do whatever work you have available."

After carefully studying our demeanor and considering our request, Mrs. Whiteside gave us our assignments. I don't recall specifically, what M.C.'s job assignment was, but my assignment was to work with Mr. Johnson, the school's janitor. He assigned me to cleaning two of the classrooms in the administration building and assisting him in cleaning the college gymnasium. We immediately started our job assignments. We reported to Mr. Johnson daily, 8am to 5pm Monday through Friday. I really enjoyed working for Mr. Johnson, as he taught me much about how to operate and handle the big commercial buffing machine that were used to mop, scrub, and sanitize the floors in the classrooms and gymnasium.

I even got a chance to go to Mr. Johnson's home and meet his wife and children. He lived near the town of Friars Point, Ms. As we worked together, he told me a lot about Clarksdale even before M.C. and I got the chance to visit the city. As we worked on our jobs we got acquainted with the physical and structural layout of the schools. We learned where president B.F. McLaurin residential quarters were and we learned where the principal's office was that was occupied by Mr. McCune.

During the weekends when we were not working, we had a lot of free time to just do whatever we could find to occupy our time. Naturally, after getting to Clarksdale and Coahoma Jr. College and securing work aid, we became increasingly curious about our surroundings. September came and the upper classmen, sophomores, came in first. The first upperclassmen we met were two young men. One was named Hilder Criss and the other young man's name was Bailey. I was curious and anxious to get to see the city of Clarksdale up close and personal. As Hilder Criss told us about the city and many of its other features, my interest was piqued even more to go to the city and visit some of its entertainment establishments for college students.

One particular Friday evening after work, Hilder requested that we go to Clarksdale with him. M.C. refused to join us, but I decided to go with him. M.C. had refused to go, because he said we didn't know enough about Hilder. Well, that simply wasn't good enough reason for me; Hilder was friendly and outgoing, and openly offered his friendship to us.

As fate dictated the outcome of that adventure, it turned out to be a bad decision. Of course, it was a poor decision on my part, not Hilder's. When we arrived in Clarksdale, he took me to a café called Black's. This place was really a 'red-light' café, better known as a juke-joint. After getting there we checked the place out, but Hilder could see my naiveté coupled with my anxiety. One of the major things he had observed about me was that I was not from a city or a town; he saw right away how anxious I was just to be in that place. Immediately, he bought us beers and played the 'Rock-Ola'— what you'd call the big music box.

There were a few people in the place, but there was an old farmer there with a younger woman, which I am certain was his lady. Well, anyone who was familiar with city life would have known that the woman was with him, or that they knew each other. I hadn't taken the necessary time to really check out the place, because my mind was preoccupied with sex.

After I had made my acquaintance with the woman by slow-dancing to two or three records by her favorite blues artists, she told me that we could go and amuse ourselves with as much sex as we could give each other, if I could be patient enough to wait until her fellow was drunk enough. Well, fate and fortune did not afford us that opportunity, because somehow her fellow sensed what we were plotting.

The old man stopped us about midway through one of those blues records. At that moment, Hilder disappeared and the woman did too! Her fellow had me collared up by my shirt and ushered me outside of that juke-joint called 'Blacks'. He reached in his farmer's overalls and pulled out a long, black pistol. He put the barrel of it against my forehead and began to lecture me about being in such a place. He commenced to tell me about myself; he said he could see immediately that I didn't belong in such a place. He also told me that I came from a good home, and that my parents had made a great sacrifice for me to be in Clarksdale to get an education from Coahoma Jr. College. But instead of me doing what I was sent there to do, I had chosen to come to a place like Black's looking for pleasure and fun.

As that old man lectured me, he pressed the barrel of the gun against my forehead and sometime my nose, just to make sure he had my full attention. This lecture must have lasted at least two to three minutes—and he made certain he had all my attention. The place was situated underneath a hill below a set of railroad tracks. I vividly recall that when he was done talking to me, my pants were messed up in the front and back! He also made me vow that once he released me, he would never, ever see me at that place again. I had enough of my wits about me to make a vow that he wouldn't see me there again, and he never did.

When he let me go, I ran every step from that place to the campus of Coahoma Jr. College. That is one of the reasons I know for a non-negotiable and indisputable fact that the college is exactly seven miles from inner city Clarksdale.

Clarksdale, Friars Point, and many of its surrounding communities were like home to me. Looking back, I can say I met some wonderful and respectable people in Clarksdale. Shortly after my encounter with Hilder Criss I met Bailey, a star quarterback for the football team. At the time Bailey and I met he was dating a pastor's daughter. Her name was Josephine Skipper. In the evenings I used to catch football passes for Bailey. We practiced running different routes after dinner. As fate would have it, he and I developed a good friendship interacting together with the football. As we continued to interact together through conversation, he told me his girlfriend had a sister. He told me her name was Bernice, and that she attended Higgins High School. At the time I was a freshman at the college, and Bernice was a senior at Higgins. One day he told me she was a cheerleader at the high school. He also told me that if I wanted to see her, go up to the high school and I would see her at cheerleader practice. I decided to oblige him and make the trip up to Higgins High School. To my amazement and surprise, I met her at the baseball field and the chemistry was instant!

We talked between embarrassing moments of shyness, awkwardness, and nervousness that normally accompany experiences of this nature. You know: the clumsiness, the running-over-your-words, the sweaty palms and the effort a young man puts forth when he is trying to impress and be the perfect gentleman; or shall I say, leave an indelible impression on a young girl. Well, I was that young man! I was so lucky, I got the chance to walk her home and also meet her parents.

Her father was the Reverend L.R. Skipper and her mother was Mrs. Willie Nell Skipper. I don't recall their address, however, at the time we met the family lived in an area of Clarksdale called Snow Ball Court. This area of Clarksdale was in the city's limits and was an exclusively African American neighborhood; it was considered the "ghetto". Thriving and struggling African Americans were relegated to substandard and meager living conditions.

While the era was a time in my life where agriculture and staple crops were the dominant order the day, it was also a time when education was the goal of any thriving and upwardly mobile African American family whether they resided in the rural areas or cities of Mississippi. The Skipper family was no exception; Bernice's father was the pastor of Chapel Hill M.B. Church in Clarksdale, Ms. The family consisted of three boys and five girls, and Bernice was the middle girl of her sisters. As I became more acquainted with her family and parents, I began to take a serious interest in their daughter. Her father was very fond of his family as well as of being the under-shepherd of Chapel Hill M.B. Church. One day shortly after I had taken a serious interest in Bernice, her father decided to give me a spelling quiz. He asked me to spell the month "February". As nervous and anxious as I was to impress him, I took on the challenge; however, in my attempt to spell the month, I left the 'r' out of my spelling. He did not scold or humiliate me. He saw the effort and the determination in me to spell the month correctly. After he had stated the month to me about three times, he then spelled and pronounced the month correctly! After my blushing embarrassment, I graciously thanked him. The greater lesson was that I never, to this day, forgot the correct pronunciation and spelling of the month of "February".

Her father and I had several conversations. I'm sure he formed his assessment of me from the effort I put forth in attempting to spell "February" correctly. Bernice's parents were very gracious, kind, and generous people. They loved their family. While they were of meager and limited material resources, they were very rich in spiritual and religious ways. I learned so much about positive human relationships from the interactions of their family, they really adopted me as their son-in-law before I ever officially asked for Bernice's hand in marriage. In a reciprocal fashion, I came to love and trust them. I wish I could count the number of times I had dinner with Bernice's family. Her mother and siblings were extremely nice and generous to me in so many ways.

I recall going to see her without a dime in my pocket. Coahoma Jr. College was seven miles from the inner city of Clarksdale, but during those times in America, you could go any place in the contiguous United States by using your thumb. Just in case you have a question about this method of traveling, it is really not complicated at all; you simply situate yourself on the side of the road with the traffic heading towards the city, town, village or state you want to go. Position yourself a safe distance on that side of the road and extend your right or left hand with your thumb pointed in that direction. If you are persistent and patient, eventually a driver will stop and give you a ride as far as they are going in that direction, if not to your destination. Every ride one was fortunate enough to get brought him or her closer to their desired goal, whatever that goal may be. These were times in America where people were more loving, kinder, more considerate, compassionate, and comforting to each other. When I think about those times in America, my heart sings songs of nostalgia. Yet my mind entertains a plethora of questions: one of major significance, 'what happened to the continuity and consistency of community?'.

I remember the time in America when race relations were not as hostile and not as maligned with the notion to annihilate an individual at the wink of an eye. As I write these words, I'm often reminded how nostalgic memories of my years in Clarksdale still revive joyful and happy feelings. And that is not a bad thing. Nostalgia, even when bittersweet, helps me to recognize my blessings at Coahoma Jr. College. It helps me look back and see how God has touched my life, and to appreciate the gifts I have received along the way.

Meeting Bernice and her family truly was a phenomenal blessing in my life. However, I must confess our relationship was fraught with challenges and obstacles. With as much time that has elapsed and the many moments of reflection, I have asked myself time and time again: was the relationship between us to be by divine providence? At this moment and juncture in my writing, I have decided not to answer that question.

Bernice had a real close girlfriend from Marks, Ms. Her name was Ann Gates. I recalled her telling me time after time that Bernice did not truly love me. I will confess, we were both high-strung, and unyielding in our personalities; I believe we both have alpha personalities. While there was a strong attraction between us, it was often difficult to determine who should dominate our relationship. Without much genuine dialogue regarding each other's real feelings, the element of fear and the lack of trust, integrity, and loyalty never got a chance to take solid root in our relationship. Let me say for the benefit of hindsight, which is always twenty-twenty vision, that at the core of us both there is still a real attraction. However, the human experience is burdened with challenges, both negative and positive. Some decisions we make for ourselves, and some others are made for us. In the final analysis, we make decisions for ourselves in life based on our overall knowledge and experiences of life. How we're socialized and acculturated in our biological families has much to do with how we feel about ourselves, how we see ourselves, and how we project our thoughts and ideas in interacting with others.

As I approached the conclusion of my two-year experience at Coahoma Jr. College in Clarksdale, I knew there would always be some experiences to be easily discarded and some that would be with me for rest of my earthly sojourn. I believe there is much to be said about an individual's personal aura. I believe when an individual is naturally imbued with an affinity for the opposite sex he or she has very little control over the outcome of who enters their life and the kind of activity generated by such encounters.

For as long as I can remember, I have always been strongly attracted to females. The other things, such as book learning, has always come fairly easy. Ultimately, I have always suffered from dealing with certain types of females in my life. I can honestly say it didn't matter how much a female admired me, there had to be a mutual attraction in order to ignite a rendezvous. I also believe that a man is structurally and anatomically built and endowed by nature to love one woman fully! I believe when Cupid shoots his arrow and it strikes its target between a man and woman— and for some reason the bond of love is severed—I believe that individual will experience a broken heart. I believe such a person will encounter all the frailties and difficulties that accompany such a devastating experience; but I also believe that life equips us with survival mechanisms called adaptation and adjustment. I believe the human being, is endowed by nature with the ability to adapt and adjust.

Mentally reviewing the concept of 'survival of the fittest' and the ability of adjustment, humans are equipped and fashioned by their Creator to go on through this mundane experience called Life—especially once they come to non-negotiable, and indisputable conclusions that "this too shall pass". I mention all this to say one of the major reasons

Bernice and I did not make it was because of a lack of trust, commitment, and devotion on both of our parts.

On the evening of my graduation from Coahoma Jr. College in May 1966, the man Bernice would eventually marry told her where I was and who I was with: my college campus girlfriend, B. Curtis. The next day around noon, this young woman and I approached the Greyhound Bus terminal so that she could get her ticket to go home. Out of nowhere, Bernice approached us both cool, calm, and collected, without a shred of excitement. Her only question to me was *why*? It has been approximately forty-nine years since Bernice asked that and a series of questions. I will confess, I didn't have the answers then and I don't have the answers now. However, I will admit, if for no other reason than a clear conscience, there is something in some men that will make them do foolish and dastardly things.

I'm sure I have been blessed and highly favored from the conception of my birth; but that does not mean I am devoid of my humanity. Every individual that occupies Planet Earth has faults. That is why we are equipped with both negative and positive qualities in our personalities. On the other hand, that is why we are challenged from God's holy word: "when we learn better, we are challenged to do better!"

I have been able to move on from my Clarksdale experiences and by the mercies and grace of God, the following September, I was able to enroll at Tennessee State University in Nashville, Tennessee. I was fortunate to remain in my chosen field of endeavor, which was Natural Science with a minor in Biology. Upon my arrival in Nashville, I joined one of my favorite classmates I'd had in Clarksdale. We became roommates for a short while. Of course, he was a veteran from DeKalb, Ms. Meridian was the closest larger city to DeKalb. Upon entering Tennessee State University, we were told who the president was, Dr. Davis. Immediately after learning who he was, almost simultaneously we were told who the president of the Science Department was; Dr.

Woods, a tall and slender, stoic-looking gentleman who taught Genetics.

Dr. Woods was chairman of the Science department. If I remember correctly his classes were Mondays, Wednesdays, and Fridays. Labs were Tuesdays and Thursdays. Dr. Woods was a skilled lecturer and a great teacher of research. Dr. John M. Malette was a professor who taught Embryology. He was very skilled and adept in his subject matter. Dr. Malette took a personal interest in my academic progress and adjustment at Tennessee State University. Dr. Johnson, who taught me Microbiology, also took a personal interest in my mastery of using the laboratory apparatus in the collection and growth of microbiological cultures in the Petri dishes. He, along with Dr. Malette, noticed my swift and exceptional ability for the study of medicine. There was also another Dr. Johnson, who taught me Kinesiology. I also had Joe Gilliam's father, who taught me Anatomy and Physiology. This is the 'Joe Gilliam' who was the first African American to get drafted by the Pittsburgh Steelers, when Terry Bradshaw was their team's quarterback. This same Joe Gilliam who had the pen-name "Jefferson Street Joe", and who was the leading quarterback for the Tennessee A & T State Tigers football team.

Big Claude Humphrey was one of their leading football players during my tenure at the University. Actually, I attended Tennessee A & T University only one year, though I have many fond memories of my time at the university. The fondest memories that still haunt my mind are ones of my days in the Science department with Dr. Malette, Dr. Woods, and both of the Drs. Johnson. These were the days when professors at Black colleges and universities took a personal interest in students, particularly if that student had potential beyond conventional measures.

I recall vividly, just before leaving the university when my grades took an instant nose dive into oblivion, Dr. Malette led the charge. He, along with Dr. Woods, Dr. Johnson and

Mr. Gilliam called me into the Science department to have a meeting and question me about my grades taking an abrupt nose dive. These professors knew my potentials. They knew my ability, and they knew that I possessed a natural affinity for the subject matter. However, they were wise enough and concerned enough to know that something personal was going on in my life. Out of their genuine caring and compassion, they stepped out of their chosen professions into the spiritual connection that unites the human family. They urged me, even went so far as to cajole and coerce me into a confession about the cause of my attitude toward my academic future. I refused to confess to my professors the real reason and the agony of my emotional pain; I decided to keep it to myself, step up, and stand up to face the real culprit: my broken heart. I went out into the city of Nashville, not far from the campus of Tennessee State University near the intersection of Sentiel and Jefferson Streets. I don't recall the name of the service station but nonetheless, I introduced myself to the owner of the station. He was a Caucasian male, and he employed me on the merits of my presentation and how I conducted myself. At that time, a person could drive into a gas station and get full service, which included pumping gasoline; checking the oil and brake fluid; checking the windshield solvent; and cleaning the vehicle's windshield. I worked for this service station long enough to get enough money to secure a round-trip bus ticket to Clarksdale. Bernice had convinced me that we could reconcile matters and make amends. We would mend our relationship and move on; however, to my astonishment, when I arrived in Clarksdale and went to her residence it was all was in vain. I stayed in Clarksdale over the weekend, but after making several telephone calls and several trips to Bernice's home, I was never able to see her. After about the third or fourth trip to her home, I remember talking with her mother. She stood in the front doorway of their home, which was located in Snowball Court in

Clarksdale. She spoke to me firmly and emphatically, without hesitation, in a voice that I remember until this day! She told me, "my daughter isn't home, Thomas." She always called me by my first name. She was a fairly tall woman in stature, with a beautiful complexion and what I call a 'Grecian gap' in her upper front teeth. I humbly responded, "yes, ma'am", and thanked her from the bottom of my heart as I turned and dismissed myself from her presence and residence. That was approximately June of 1967.

I turned and walked to the Greyhound Bus terminal and boarded a bus back to Nashville. I stayed in Nashville and managed to remain employed long enough to earn money to send my large travelling trunk and suitcases on Greyhound to Memphis. It must have been mid-August 1967 when I took my farewell trip out of Nashville to return to Durant, Mississippi. I must have arrived in Durant about 4pm or 5:30pm on a Friday evening. Upon my arrival I was fortunate enough to get a ride from Durant to Long Branch, which was approximately seven miles northwest of the city of Durant.

My father's home and property were situated between Lexington and the town of West. As has already been mentioned, my father was a Baptist preacher and he was also pastor of four Baptist churches. Upon my arrival home, my father was finishing a weekly revival in a little town between Sallis, Mississippi and Kosciusko called McCool. However, before my father came home from McCool, I had arrived home about 5:30-6:00pm that same Saturday afternoon. As you might imagine, my mother was visibly upset when I entered our home with all of my suitcases and big trunk. I greeted my mother in my usual voice. Let me just say, as fond as my mother was of me and as much as she loved me, neither she nor my father were people of open or lavish affection—not even when they were pleased with their children's accomplishments. You can imagine how they were when they were displeased. Be that as it is, the fact remained that my mother was visibly disappointed and seriously displeased at my coming home with all of my belongings.

When my mother dropped her head and grunted, the sound seemed as though it came from her soul. No matter how hurt or disappointed she was, she'd always managed to at least hear my side of the story; even if I was lying. And so, after the initial shock of my story she'd mustered up that compassion, that tenderness, and that tolerance only a mother has for her child. No matter what my story was, somehow or another, she'd put on that happy face for me, if for no other reason than to get all of my story. She gently consoled and goaded me until she'd gotten all of the story from all angles. Then, we'd discussed a plausible and feasible solution before Papa got home.

I am sure my mother's and my relationship was so unique and strange, she could direct, manipulate and maneuver me into figuring out what was best for me; and yet at the same time, allow me to feel as though I had come up with the solution myself. Only a mother who is endowed with a loving heart full of God's grace and mercy could guide such a rebellious, frustrated, confused, and immature prodigal son back to the path—the path that is essential to reap the benefits of a well-prepared and productive life.

My father came home about midnight that Friday night and immediately after arriving home, he heard my voice. He asked my mother, "is that that boy's voice I hear?"Hesitantly, my mother answered very cautiously! My father quickly inquired as to why I was home. As best she could, my mother summarized for him what she and I had talked about. He permitted her to explain for maybe five to eight minutes; I happened to be in an adjoining room next to their room. I was not asleep, because I was still in quite a dilemma and experiencing a wide range of emotions contrary to what a normal young man should be experiencing at that stage in his life. After my father had heard enough from my mother about my being home he abruptly said to her, "I'll get him up about five o'clock in the morning", which was a Saturday morning. He further added, "he and I will have a talk as we go out to the field and pull up a few cockle-burrs from the cotton in that six-acre's bottom".

True to his word, he called out my name around five in the morning. Of course, I answered with some reluctance and hesitation. He said, "son, let's you and I go out to the cotton field for a little while."

"Yes, sir!," I quickly replied.

We got out into the six-acres bottom, which was filled with cotton. There was nothing but cotton as far as my eyes could see, however the cotton had an unwanted plant that grew in it called the 'cockle-burr'. This plant grew among the cotton as an undesirable, aggravating and uncontrollable plant. The plant grew seeds that were aggravating and repulsive to anyone who attempted to cultivate or harvest the cotton at the appropriate time. Its burrs were not only a hindrance and nuisance to people, but to animals as well. When the plant was about seventy-percent mature—before it produced the irritating seeds that caught on to human beings and animals as well—the farmer and his family would take the initiative and physically pull as many of the plants from his field as possible before the actual harvest.

So, as my father started to pull up these plants, he and I had a nice and relaxed conversation going. Now, I don't really recollect what we were talking about; but I will tell you it was small talk in comparison to the main topic, which was the real reason I was home from Tennessee A & I State University. As we proceeded with the small talk, he abruptly switched the conversation with lightning speed to the real question: why I was really here. When he made the question direct and pointed, I immediately began searching for the best answer that I thought was straightforward yet suitable for the forthcoming prophetic explanation given me by my father.

Frankly, I told him Bernice and I had broken up, separated as boyfriend and girlfriend. He then asked me what was my plan going forward. I was lost, confused and simply broken and yet understandably so; I was naïve, immature, gullible and inexperienced in every phase of life. He knew that I was coming into manhood with hormones coursing all through my body. He also knew from the crazy and uncouth answer I gave him that my explanation was irrational and erratic in every sense of the word. I said I was going to Kansas City, Kansas, because I had heard the popular song that was on all the radio stations. *"Pretty women in Kansas City, Kansas City here I come!"*

I was amazed at how my father was able to totally pick my mind before he gave me what I called a life-changing prophecy that reoriented and redirected my entire life at that time. He prefaced his response with almost these exact words:

"Son, have you got a moment?"

"Yes, sir!", was my response. Then he carefully chose the appropriate words to say exactly what I needed to hear. Let me say parenthetically, only a father and a son could have had this conversation:

"You need to give some serious thought to completing your education; because by the turn of the century, fathers are going to be killing their sons and sons are going to be killing their fathers. Mothers are going to be killing their daughters, and daughters are going to be killing their mothers. Son, it is going to be extremely hard for those that have an education to survive; I don't even want to think about those that have no education. About the turn of the century, water will be a commodity for sale. Son, I will not be here! And son, I don't want to be here, because to survive is going to be a 'rat race'!"

When my father finished his conversation with me I was totally transformed. In fact, the conversation was so mind-boggling I was semi-comatose. With the final words of our conversation he said, "son, you might want to think about what I have just said to you."

I was literally in a state of shock, because that was the very first time my father and I had had that kind of conversation since I'd been on the planet. And yet, it was a 'rite of passage' conversation from boyhood to manhood. One thing was sure, he knew he had totally captured and commanded my full attention.

Now, my father chewed tobacco and smoked cigarettes too. When he was done talking to me, we pulled up a few more cockle-burrs from the cotton field. I distinctly remember that Saturday morning, because the following Sunday he had to go to Water Valley, Ms. To his First Sunday church. The name of that church was Spring Hill Missionary Baptist. That was the first church he had been called to pastor. My father was very fond of the parishioners of that church. It was a long way from our home in Long Branch. I would venture to say Spring Hill M.B. Church was approximately 100 miles away. My father would get up about 4:00am to get dressed every First Sunday morning. He would leave home about 6:00am headed to Water Valley in order to get there to start Sunday school at 10:00am. My father was dedicated and committed to the service of his four churches.

When he left for his First Sunday church following our conversation, I went up to the barn. The barn was a building where he kept harvest grain such as corn and other farming equipment. Two side stables were built onto it where we kept livestock such as mules and horses that were used to cultivate the fields. In the top of that barn just below the roof was space for storing hay and other necessary food other than ears of corn. There was ample space where one could get away from the hustle and the vicissitudes of life to think and meditate.

When my father left for Water Valley early that First Sunday headed to Spring Hill M.B. Church, I did not accompany him. I was thinking about the greatest and heaviest conversation my father and I had ever had during my entire adult life. I clearly remember my mother saying to me, "are you going with your father today?"

"No ma'am, Mama", I said.

"Are you going to Sunday school at the family church?", she asked, referring to Long Branch Missionary Baptist Church. My response was an emphatic "no, ma'am!" to both questions. I recall finally saying to her, "Mama, I just need some time to myself."

Well, as you might imagine, all mothers know their children. My mother may not have known the particulars of the conversation with my father; but she was wise enough to observe from my mannerisms and disposition that whatever the content of our conversation was, it had certainly left an indelible impression not only in my mind, but in my entire being. I said to my mother, "Mama, I am going to spend the rest of the day meditating and reflecting on what I want to do for the rest of my life."

During that day, as you might imagine, several things came into my mind. One of the things that stayed in my mind was continuing my college career.

When my father got home from Water Valley, as was his custom, he and my mother discussed the church service. Then of course, my mother's next move was to prepare his meal. While she prepared his dinner, she would also tell him how we had behaved. Clearly and succinctly, she would report to him about the conduct and behavior of each of us. Provided he was satisfied with the report, his next move was reading the newspaper. Once he started reading the weekly Memphis Commercial Appeal newspaper, it would take him approximately two to three hours to do a thorough job of reading it. My point is, if anyone had a request to make of him, you had better do it before he got into reading his newspaper. Well, I decided to interrupt him and make my request.

As I approached him very carefully and reluctantly, my question was succinct and to the point. I led into my question with a question:

"Papa, will you do me a favor?," I asked.

"Son, you know I will if I can. What is it you want?"

"Will you take me to Greenwood, Mississippi?"

Surprisingly, his reply was "yes...what is in Greenwood?"

"Well, I want you to take me to Mississippi Valley State College," I told him.

He really wasn't surprised then, so he pretended. He called my mother in on the big question:

"Jannie, you hear what this boy is asking me?," Papa said.

Of course, it was like a prepared and rehearsed script!

"No, Jake," my mother said. What did he ask?"

"He said he wants to go over to Greenwood to that college over there."

My mother took the initiative, saying, "well, if he says he wants to go over there, why you go ahead and take him."

"Well, you know I don't have any money," my father said.

At that point, I took the initiative.

"Well Papa, all I want you to do is take me to the college," I said.

At that point where the question of finance was not the central issue of the matter, the discussion was really over. It was just a matter of me getting my school materials and clothes together, and making preparation for Mississippi Valley State University, which was in Itta Bena, Mississippi.

CHAPTER FIVE

My father and I took the trip to Itta Bena to the campus of Mississippi Valley State College in August of 1967. As I remember, it was a Monday morning when we left our Long Branch community home. My father had a 1953 Chevrolet with a manual transmission. Now, my father did drive his cars first, which means he never drove any faster than 30-35 mph. The city of Greenwood was approximately sixty or seventy-five miles one way from our home, and Itta Bena was approximately six or eight miles from the city limits of Greenwood located on Highway #82 West going toward Greenville. We left home for Greenwood about 8:30am, and we must have reached the campus of Mississippi Valley State College at approximately 11am or 12am. The young men's dormitory was located adjacent to the campus dining hall.

When I continued my college career in August of 1967 at Mississippi Valley State College, I stepped out totally and unequivocally, leaning on the grace, mercy, love, and wisdom of God. I came from a dysfunctional environment and a home with a plethora of family problems; yet, there were several fundamental structures in place to sustain and validate a loving home where the presence of God resided at all times. Even with many doubts invading my mind, in the midst of all the negatives I still had a mother's love and the stern hand of a strong father's discipline whispering in my ears, *'go on, boy, you're here now and you can make it.'* With those words of affirmation ringing in my ears and fire in my soul, I hit Mississippi Valley State College like a tornado!

And so, as fate would have it these two young men, Willie G. McGaha and Terrell Chapman observed me standing in the parking lot with my trunk, all of my clothing, and materials for school. After they saw me struggling and in distress, out of curiosity they came to my rescue. Now mind you, they were coming from the dining hall going back to their room in the men's dormitory. They came to me and introduced themselves, and instantly we became friends. They invited me to their room in the men's dormitory and we sat around and talked for perhaps an hour or so. After we had gotten better acquainted as I shared my story, their hearts reached out to mine. After I had really informed them of my story, sparing no details, these fellows instantly reached out to me from their souls. I told them I had no money and no immediate financial resources; these fellows put their heads together and devised a plan. They made an agreement among the three of us, overriding the sentiment of the other two fellows whom I had not met that also resided in the room. Terrell's and Willie's decisions to allow me to stay in their room illegally overpowered the other fellows' decisions. Before my National Defense loan was granted from the government to complete my Education degree, there was plenty of ducking, dodging, and plenty of lying, scheming and hiding, as you might imagine. It took almost one year before my National Defense loan was approved.

Back in the day, I made several visitations to the Business Office, making good faith promises that their money was coming. Frankly, the Business Office at Mississippi Valley State University demonstrated enough faith in my efforts and on the strength of my promise that their finances would be secured. Out of that encounter with two young men I'd met as I stood in the parking lot with my personal belongings, a lifetime friendship was forged among the three of us.

One of the things I quickly recognized and understood in interacting and competing with my classmates in the Science department, my previous academic preparation at Coahoma Jr. College and Tennessee State University had catapulted me miles ahead of my classmates. Many of the Science courses in my allotted regime of coursework were repetitious. Since I had already had many of the courses, that made my experience less challenging in the pursuit of my degree. Consequently, with ample time afforded to me, there was time to be utilized in other areas of my life; so, I became very popular with the ladies. I had quite a few friends and girlfriends on the campus. As good fortunes afforded me, I had two sisters that were graduates of Mississippi Valley State College prior to my matriculation. My youngest sister, who had attended MVSC and graduated before me, had gotten married and taught Physical Education at Coleman High School in Greenville. She had left quite a reputation on the campus. While she was attending the University, she ran for "Ms. Mississippi Valley State College Homecoming Queen." With that kind of recognition and notoriety, she had left an easy and enjoyable path for me to travel.

And so, as you might imagine, I had friends and acquaintances from one end of the campus to the other. I must add, I wasn't a 'dead-head' either, book-wise. To study Science and be a member of the department was quite an honor in and of itself; not to mention graduation. My journey at MVSC was quite an interesting saga. Early during my journey, my sister introduced me to this one physician from Newport News, Virginia, Dr. J.B.Y.; I will give his initials rather than be presumptuous about using his name. Let me just say, "Doc", as the people of Greenville fondly called him, was quite a fellow and friend.

As I reflect on our friendship, Doc was quite fond of the ladies. He was a graduate of Meharry Medical School in Nashville, Tennessee. I frequently accompanied him on several medical meetings and conventions in Nashville. Even in Greenville, he had his share of ladies. He had an apartment he called his 'after-hours playhouse'. He had a complete stock of the best wines and liquors; simply stated, the best alcoholic beverages were kept in his after-hours apartment. Being that I was his friend, my two best college friends, Willie and Terrell were also privileged to the best of jazz music and other entertainment. As you might imagine, there was nothing on the planet to compare to that unbridled freedom given to us three young college 'jocks'.

That was quite a lot of access and unrestricted privilege to that kind of life at our ages, considering that we were country boys in origin. Since I was in my senior year he gave me a key to the place, which really made bad matters worse! Can you imagine three young country boys exposed to and experiencing that kind of life? It's beyond any earthly description. Yet, for all Doc's blatant and open permission to use his apartment and supply of entertainment and alcoholic beverages, he still kept a watchful eye over us. We only dealt with the ladies he recommended, not just any ladies indiscriminately. And yes, they were women without discretion; they willingly participated in the activities that life offered. Those memories flood my mind as I think on yesteryear.

'Back in the day', there was the band director Mr. A, and his better half, Mrs. A.A., was extremely beautiful and attractive. Every time I see a picture of Gabrielle Union, my fantasy sweetheart, I think of Mrs. A.A. She was a native of Greenville, and she was astonishingly beautiful. We never had sexual relations, but I know the mutual desire was there; the circumstances never availed the opportunity. I walked away from the experience knowing that there are some 'roses' in the female human family that are too beautiful to be plucked.

I leave this saga of my life with thought and reflections of another beautiful and attractive young lady that I encountered. She also was a native of Greenville, and her initials are M.P. This young lady and I had a strong sexual attraction for each other. We had several encounters, yet we never had a social and communicative relationship. She was a very wonderful and sweet person to share sexual and good spiritual energy. We would hook up with each other without any verbal communication. Our bodies would connect in ecstasy for hours, seemingly! Let me conclude this portion of my college career by mentioning a young lady from Cleveland, Mississippi. Her initials are M.J. I left her at

MVSU. By the time we hooked up and started to date, the University name had changed from Mississippi Valley State College to Mississippi Valley State University. I am sure the name was officially changed in 1969. I don't recall what M.J.'s major was at the university, but I can tell you she loved herself some 'Jake'. [Jake is my pen name!] Then there was also G.R. of Yazoo. Ms. G.R. and I were dating when I graduated; the last contact we had, she was residing in Georgia. She had a wonderful and loving family. She also had one brother, his name was E.R.

In all fairness and honesty, I also met a beautiful and spiritually wonderful young lady while attending MVSU by the name of G.G. To this day I'm not certain what her major was, though I believe it was Nursing. G.G. had family that had attended the university prior to my matriculation. I do recall that she and I had some of the same instructors in the Science department. One whom I specifically remember was Mr. Silas Peyton, who taught us Anatomy and Physiology. At that time, Mr. Peyton was also an exchange professor at Delta State University in Cleveland, Mississippi. As I recall, Delta State University had just begun a student integration exchange trial program between the two universities. Ms. Valley State University was an African American university and Delta State was a Caucasian university.

Students began to attend our university, although racial tensions were high and sometimes explosive. I recalled during the fall of 1968 when Stokely Carmichael, H. 'Rap' Brown, and Eldridge Cleaver were traversing the south with the message of 'Black Power'. Frequently, civil unrest was prevalent in many urban cities and university campuses across the deep South. The civil rights movement caused much of the violence and chaos in the deep South. The ripple effect spread far and wide in the cities and colleges in the deep south. Consequently, Delta State University and MVSU were no exception. G.G's family knew the Fitzgerald family in Natchez before Armstrong Rubber Works hired me as an employee. G.G. and I were infatuated and attracted to each other prior to my going to Natchez for employment; of course, by me accepting employment there made it really convenient for us to see each other more. Actually, G.G. was seeing and in love with another fella whose name I don't recall. I believe they got married and I believe she had a child for him; however, in G.G.'s heart there was always a place for me. I say that with as much conviction as I can muster, however, fate dictated otherwise for her and me. G.G. was a very special person to me. There was a deep spiritual connection between the two of us. G.G. fondly called me by my pen name 'Jake'. As I reflect on our relationship, nobody could call my name and stir me quite like her. She gave me a wrist bracelet with an engraved inscription: *"never lose love"*. I kept that bracelet for a long time; however, G.G. made her transition in the nineties. I recall my sister telling me about it, and I whispered a prayer that her soul was well-received into eternity.

My next passionate and compelling saga that jogs my memory was D. Thornbird, a young woman with two daughters and a sister. I don't recall either her daughters' nor her sister's names. However, the relationship between us was passionate, explosive, fiery, and unpredictable.

Ms. D. Thornbird was a good woman; but she was a liar. She told me she attended Coppin College in Baltimore, Maryland. She tried everything she could to get right for me, but it just was not there, other than physically. One thing I found out about her also, she was a 'bigamist'. I also know her ex-husband worked on the riverboats that traveled up and down the Mississippi River between New Orleans and Memphis, Tennessee. Finally, these are flames and relationships that occurred in my life with women before I met Ms. G. H.

My days at Mississippi Valley State University in Itta Bena will forever be etched on the pages of my conscience. It's funny; if you were to ask me our areas of study or college majors, I honestly believe I could not tell you. I know that my friend Willie McGaha, who was from Rienzi, Mississippi, got married to his college sweetheart, Olivia. She told me he went into the United States Armed Forces; I believe it was there he made a career. About twenty years ago, he made his transition. Our other friend Terrell Chapman, who was a native of Hollingdale, Mississippi, also went into the United States Armed Forces. Subsequent to the completion of his service, he became a Registered Pharmacist. He also married his high school sweetheart, Jean Chapman, who attended Jackson State University. Professionally, she is a psychologist. Currently, they reside in Memphis. They were blessed to have two daughters.

During my one year and a summer at Mississippi Valley State University I completed my undergraduate degree with a major in Natural Science and a minor in Biology. My academic year and summer were filled with lots of adventure and academic excitement. Among the many exhilarating and memorable challenges, I vividly remember Dr. Clay Simpson, who taught me and two other interesting and intelligent fellows, Willie Blair and Richard Watson. The three of us carried the academic mantle in Microbiology. During that time, the Rockefeller and Rhodes Foundations sent scouts throughout Mississippi to its various African American universities seeking potential candidates who possessed the scholastic aptitude to study medicine. When the scouts entered Dr. Simpson's Microbiology class they made an inquiry regarding a potential candidate or candidates. After Dr. Simpson welcomed them to the class and briefly engaged them regarding what they were seeking, he recommended Richard Watson and Willie Blair with much fervor and enthusiasm. However, when he called my name, he said, "Thomas J. McClellan can do it, but I don't think he has the discipline!" To my amazement and surprise, that statement never left my mind—even after graduating from college and starting a career in a field of science that dealt primarily with private industry, Armstrong Tires and Rubber Works in Natchez, Mississippi.

Simply called 'the tire plant' by the local residents of the city, I would conservatively estimate that this plant employed about three thousand people. The primary function of this industry was the production and supply of rubber tires for any and all machines that had a need for its products. My tenure at Armstrong's Rubber Works was brief in duration. Being restless, immature, and lacking in experience in all areas of my life, it would be fair to conclude that I was searching for my boundaries in life as well as finding my best purpose.

It did not take very long at Armstrong's Tire and Rubber Works to discover that I was not suited for that line of work. Being Apache Choctaw Indian, African, and Irish by heritage and growing up in a segregated community in the American deep South, had much to do with my restless and self-determined drive to leave the South. I had been taught to be complacent and submissive; yet there was strong yearning in my being that compelled and propelled my inner nature to seek a better place where I could find peace and contentment for myself.

CHAPTER SIX

Now that I reflect on my total persona at that time, my self-esteem was at rock bottom. My thinking was dark and negative in most areas of my life. After much self-evaluation, interacting with others, and also experiencing education in institutions of higher learning my overall assessment of myself has changed and continues in a self-evolving state of flux. Consequently, I have become positive, motivated, and optimistic; especially since I have been reading Norman Vincent Peale's books and every issue of 'Guideposts' I can get into my hands. As a matter of fact, reading is a habit that energizes my life and fires up my enthusiasm and commitment to helping others. My ambition and aim in writing my autobiography is to share my life experiences with others.

The professions and vocations where I have served still currently serve my overall objective. I am a tri-cultured individual and still experience an insurmountable number of obstacles, yet I persevere. In my efforts and determination to leave the deep South I sought better employment opportunities and better social and civic race relations. As I reflect on my adventures and yearning desire to move from the deep South to the cities of Chicago, Illinois and Gary, Indiana, I am not certain they were all I thought they would be, or all I had expected. Now that I have had the benefit of several experiences I believe my efforts to evolve, grow, and mature to where I am now have been phenomenal. I approach my life journey this way because through it all, life has taught me that God's grace, mercy, understanding, and compassion has been abundant in my life from the onset. As I think about it, I have no reservation in stating that once upon a time in my life, my emotions were distorted, my will was deadened, and my efforts were focused in a worldly direction. Even then, God was with me.

Before I get too far in discussing my life pursuits in Chicago, Illinois and Gary, Indiana, I must admit I thought I had met the love of my life in Natchez, Mississippi. Her name was Gloria H. I was introduced to her family through my sister who taught at Sadie V. Thompson Elementary School in Natchez. My sister, Mrs. Nannie C. McClellan Fitzgerald and her husband, Mr. Will T. Fitzgerald had one child, Dr. Lynette Althea Fitzgerald Alexis. Lynette currently practices medicine at one of the local hospital in Fort Worth, Texas.

I know it may sound strange and rather far-fetched; but by the time I met Ms. Gloria H. I was ready to do some serious talking about a family and a future. However, as I reflect on the entire Natchez saga, I am certain that I foolishly pursued dangerous people and things God told me in His word to avoid. But because of His love for me, I have come to the conclusion God is the master of the adventure of living, and following His wisdom has led me to the fullness of my life.

Gloria H., whom my sister introduced me to, was a graduate of Southern University in Scotlandville, Louisiana. To this day, I never knew what Gloria's major was in college. I don't know; I guess I never thought to ask her. I will say her father was name Mr. C. H. and her mother was name Mrs. M. H. Gloria had a sister name "Nette" and her brother was fondly called 'Mickey'. Gloria's family had their own family business. Her father had a 'bump shop'; its primary objective was to repair wrecked and damaged cars and trucks that had been in accidents. Gloria's family was an urban 'bourgie' family. They were the 'shakers and movers' of Natchez's upscale community, if there was one—depending on who you were talking to about the era and urban growth of Natchez at that time. Gloria's family was close-knit and of a Creole genealogy. In my opinion, Natchez was a town that was closely knit in its social hierarchy and very resistant to others who were not a "homegrown" product of the community; outsiders were not well-accepted in the city. To say the least, these were my experiences during my entire time in the city, and especially interacting with its citizenry. Upon entering the city, there is a statue of Jefferson Davis welcoming all visitors to the "cradle of the Confederacy" where the true south still lives. I can tell you, that slogan wreaked havoc on my psyche, and during my entire work experience in the city I was repulsed and insulted by it—yet I never shared that with anyone. Even then it was appalling and amazing to me how African Americans [Negroes] could be so happy and oblivious to subtle discriminatory acts. They would go about their daily occupations and professions as if everything was alright. And yes, in their minds, things were alright, because their daily conversations and pursuits centered around who could get a job at the plant, International Paper Company, or the chemical company called "Thikoil". The local entertainment bar in Natchez at the time was the White House. As the night progressed and your appetite and thirst hungered for more food or alcoholic beverages, you simply left Natchez and went to Vidalia, Louisiana to a club called Danny's. Danny's had everything you needed as far as alcohol and live entertainment. Then there was Babe's, a café/hotel structure for your conjugal and food needs, providing you so desired.

Natchez provided many of the things I desired in my life at that age; but to be honest, even then I was in search of a good, moral, and respectful wife. My approach and my search may have been in the wrong places and directions. However, that does not negate the fact that I was still, in a subconscious and a subliminal way, expecting to have a good wife and family. There were so many times I thought I had found her in the women I met and had relationships with; but such was not the case, even with Gloria, whom I grew to care for deeply. Personally, I feel we never fully connected because we never really got to know each other. It is extremely difficult for two high-strong and strong-willed people to be compatible. An alpha-male and an alpha-

95

female...well, much can be said, and many conversations discussed about the likelihood of success for such a union.

Frankly, Gloria and I never got to know each other mentally and emotionally. Clearly, Gloria was a Daddy's girl; she looked just like her father facially and she was very subtle and controlling in her behavior and mannerisms. Truthfully, I have no problems with a young lady possessing any of those features or characteristics. However, in dealing with or being in a relationship with me, the relationship must be democratic in its structure. I have never needed a woman to think *for* me; of course, I have no problems with her thinking *with* me. I believe in and advocate a dialogue and mutual respect as part of the core values of marriage. I recall a young man telling me a long time ago, there are three things that are primary in a marital relationship: sex, food, and respect—in any arrangement one chooses. I have learned I don't have to like you to respect you; but I cannot respect you unless I like you.

Communication, in my opinion, is key in any relationship. I don't care if it's platonic or romantic, there must be communication in order for the relationship to thrive and survive. I have further learned that you cannot earn or demand another's love. Love must occur spontaneously and naturally, and it must also be rooted and grounded in a power higher than mundane or earthly levels. I have learned and come to accept that love must be the foundation for the longevity of any relationship of substance. It's never is and never has been about the love of power in a genuine relationship of substance; but instead, the power of love predicated on 1st Corinthians, thirteenth chapter.

I have had to experience the struggles, agony, and bitterness of defeat before I could receive the fruit and wisdom that were inherent in each town where I have resided. In each place I have been and spent valuable time, I have obtained valuable and incredible wisdom that was beneficial to my life in a positive way.

As you may have concluded by now, fate and time determined that Gloria and I would not make it as lovers. One evening in early September of 1970 she and I were in downtown Natchez, talking about the condition at Armstrong Rubber Works. The company was on strike, and company employees were required to do the hourly workers' jobs until the labor dispute was resolved and the hourly employees returned to work. Our conversation was centered around my agony and frustration of having to do their jobs along with other company employees. Abruptly, as daring and bold as she was in her own devious way, she pulled her dress up to the apex of her beautiful, luscious thighs, revealing the crest of her vagina. Then she said to me in a daring and facetious way, "Thomas, you cannot leave Natchez because this is what you want." Frankly speaking, she didn't realize at the moment how right she was; however, little did she know one of my best qualities was that I didn't respond to the way she threatened me. I quickly concluded that she did not know me at all! If memory serves me correctly, I believe I remained in Natchez only long enough to give Armstrong final notice that I was relocating. I then went to U-Haul and rented a small U-Haul trailer and hitch and hooked it onto my 1970 GTO Pontiac. I put all of my clothes and belongings in it, then went to my sister's home for a departing conversation with her and her family. To this day I have never revealed truthfully to them why I left Natchez. Oh, they pleaded, and questioned me in every way one could possibly be interrogated. I have yet to tell them the real reason, along with being laid off from Armstrong and the dating encounter with Gloria.

Frankly, the moment Gloria did that to me, something in me instantly died for her. It did not die at that very moment, but it was a process. I had always questioned her integrity, ethics, and virtue. I know; perhaps you have now concluded that I am a dual-standard man. And that is okay; justifiably or unjustifiably, I am culturally a product of the village. My suspicions served me well with Gloria. As beautiful and well-endowed as she was physically, she was not the permanent one for me. I may have been ever-so-infatuated and stunned by her physical attributes, but most importantly, we did not connect spiritually. In my opinion, her sister 'Nette and I connected better than she and I did. Gloria had a devious, subtle and cunning nature; for whatever reasons, she wasn't very forthright and deliberate. I seriously believe Gloria was an enigma even to herself. Lastly, my suspicions and 'sixth sense' were finally confirmed when I visited Natchez to see her and my family. I was wearing a cat-eye diamond ring on my pinky finger. She requested that ring, and I gave it to her. I later learned from a reliable source that she had given it to her lover—the same fellow she was dealing with when I was working there, and long after I'd journeyed on to Chicago, Illinois and Gary, Indiana. I later learned they had a daughter together.

After relocating to Chicago and Gary, it was really difficult to find employment doing anything—even with my college degree. I thoroughly remember attempting to find employment at several places, but my efforts were to no avail. I was reading several newspaper want ads, but a decent job was difficult to find.

I distinctly remember living with my mother's youngest sister, Aunt Jesse M. Johnson, who resided at 2588 Delaware Street in Gary. My aunt allowed me to room with her at a cost of $32 dollars a month. She made it crystal-clear to me, though: I could stay there, but she would not cook my meals. She was charging me to sleep there and store my belongings and clothes. Now my oldest sister, Mrs. Inez Jones and brother-in-law Mr. Berry Jones lived at 4044 South State Street in the Robert Taylor Projects in Chicago. As you might imagine, I was back and forth between my aunt's house in Gary and my sister's apartment in Chicago.

I arrived in Chicago from Natchez in late August or early September of 1970. Before I left for Chicago, I decided to visit my alma mater, Mississippi Valley State University, one last time. While visiting the campus I ran into my old buddy and ex-roommate, Terrell Chapman. I grabbed him up and we took a drive to my home in Durant. I introduced my old buddy and best friend to my parents then I took him back to MVSU in Itta Bena. That was the last time I visited my old alma mater. Following that visit, I took Highway 82 East to Highway 51 North, which was a straight shot into Memphis. From there I went to St. Louis and finally into Chicago. Being young and adventurous, my curiosity and energy level was extremely high. I was young, loose and carefree, with no responsibility; *look out, world, here I come!* With as little as I knew about the north, my anxious and inquiring mind was in for a rude awakening. Although I had a college degree, employment wasn't as easy to secure as I had thought.

Little did I know, I had entered an entirely different world, culturally speaking. Being totally ignorant and naïve of how the world operates, I didn't realize I'd entered a world contrary to what I'd been born and raised in. Consequently, that took some assimilation, and certainly some adaptation on my part. Being young and just out of college with very limited experience beyond my Mississippi roots, it was a challenge; but you can best believe that it wasn't too long before I was up to speed and off and running to employment in East Chicago, Illinois.

East Chicago was about fifteen or twenty miles east of Gary, Indiana. My first job was with a company called Inland Steel Company. As you may know, the East Chicago and Gary areas are plentiful with a variety of steel mills. Arriving in the cities of Chicago and Gary straight out of Mississippi with a college degree, I clearly thought it would not take more than a week or two before I was gainfully employed by some industry. But little did I know, there is a school called Life; the experiences of life quickly taught me that, regardless of who you are—and especially being an African American male—there are lessons in this life that are exclusively and categorically for *you.*

The degrees one has attained, or his pedigree didn't always matter. Being an African American male, you quickly learned the structure and hierarchy of the American system. You quickly learned that book literacy had its place in the broader scheme of the system's functioning capacity; however, the economic and political structure did not necessarily align with justice and equality for you in its distribution of goods and services, with respect to employment.

And so, after much effort, fraught with disappointment and the agony of defeat, I landed a job working at Inland Steel Mill working near a blast furnace. My job was to catch the 25-foot long 'H' bars of steel, which weighed about five hundred pounds. When these bars dropped out of the blast furnace and onto a flat bed of rollers, my job was to position myself at the end of the roller bed with a long hand tool similar to a pitchfork and keep them in a straight line until they made it completely across the bed to the cooling trays. This job came about just as I was getting ready to leave the cities of Chicago and Gary and return to Natchez. I remember the day as if it was yesterday.

I was in my 1970 Pontiac GTO and I drove up to a Sunoco service station on 25th and Broadway in Gary. As I began complaining to the service station attendant, who was African American about how difficult it was to find a job, he said to me, "have you considered Inland Steel Company in East Chicago?" I told me no; he told me to at least give them a try before going back to Natchez. I took the brother's advice and fortunately, Inland Steel Co. employed me!

Shortly after I was employed, I began to pay my debts. I owed my uncles in Gary, my mother's brothers. While I was seeking employment, my money would run short from time to time, and I would borrow money from two of my uncles when I ran short. One of my uncles loaned me money without interest; but one loaned me money *with* interest, specifically, twenty-five cents on a dollar.

Shortly after becoming employed at Inland Steel, the public-school system of Gary employed me. The personnel director was Mr. Vann Humbrick. After our very pleasant interview he informed me that he had an opening in the middle school called Beckman Jr. High School, adjacent to Roosevelt High School located on Grant Street. Mr. Jasper Sykes was principal and Mr. Nelson was assistant principal. My assignment was 7th and 8th grade science levels. I must admit, it was quite a transition to go from industry to teaching and training young children. I enjoyed it; it posed quite a challenge and change in my demeanor as well as my overall outlook on life.

As I mentioned earlier in the writing of this book, my mother's people were not fond of my father and his people. When they left Mississippi for better jobs and employment opportunities, my father did not join them in transitioning from the south to the north. My mother's entire immediate family moved from Mississippi to Gary, Indiana. They moved to Gary to work in the steel mills—in which all of my mother's brothers were employed. They settled there, and most of them purchased their own homes. My mother chose to stay with her husband and her children, and in so doing created a deeper rift in her family against my father and his family. Admittedly, there was animosity and division between the families from the onset. However, my mother and father chose to stay with each other and have their children, and accept the challenges of their marriage to raise, provide, and educate their children to the best of their ability. They have been deceased for a number of years now; but I can tell you I am extremely grateful for the choice they made in staying together as husband and wife and dedicating their lives to us as a family, in the only way they knew. As I write this book and reflect, I am certain of the undying and committed love they had for each other. If not for that, the marriage couldn't have lasted and sustained the challenges it encountered.

I mention all of that to address the negativity I encountered from my aunt and uncles when they met and congregated at my aunt's house at 2588 Delaware Street in Gary. Shortly after arriving in Gary, my mother had arranged my rooming and boarding with my Aunt Jessie. My aunt's husband had been deceased for years. Aunt Jessie allowed me to rent a room from her for thirty-two dollars a month; that what was she called 'boarding'. Now, she had me to understand clearly that there was no cooking involved. From time to time, of course, she would decide at her discretion to offer me a meal. My aunt was the type of woman who would assign odd jobs to me and expected me to do them in addition to the assigned thirty-two dollars board I was assessed. I had an older brother who had lived with her prior to my staying with her. I am certain she realized the mistake she made with me; as she would so often state, "you don't have a bit of your brother in you; when I'd tell him to do a job, he would jump and do it!'

My response was, "yes, Aunt Jessie, that was *him*. I ain't him. And I have told you time and time again, I don't do odd jobs. I am not a handy man. I am going to pay you your 32 dollars a month for my staying here, and that is all you're going to get from me!"

It took a few months of my staying with her before she finally accepted that I meant what I said. But I can tell you and few other people, she finally got it—and I can testify, she has never forgotten it and never allowed me to live it down! Currently, my Aunt Jessie is over one hundred years of age. All of my uncles and aunts on both my father's and my mother's side are deceased except Aunt Jessie. As I write this book, she is now residing in Simmons Loving Care Health Facility in Gary.

 While we had a tumultuous and stormy relationship, she taught me invaluable lessons about the culture and the

102

people of Gary. Really, our relationship was both sweet and bitter—a combination of salt and pepper in description. Even back then, my aunt was an extremely liberated and feminist woman. She worked for the public-school Board of Education in the sanitation department. She was a janitor by vocation and took great pride in her job. She worked very diligently and faithfully on her job. Like any other working organization, they too had their cliques and gossiping group.

I must admit there was a great bias on my mother's side of the family because of their strong dislike and negative attitude towards my father. Because of that general attitude throughout the family, it naturally affected the disposition and attitude of the children. This was an ongoing, simmering, monstrous demon that lurked under the surface of our family interactions; from time to time as tensions grew, it would rear its head. It has scarred and affected the family in a general and dysfunctional way until this day. With that confession, let me address my specific dilemma with "Aunt" and "Uncles" from the time of my arrival in the city of Gary. With my genealogy being as it is, I clearly had no choice in the selection of my parents. My extended family's insensitivities, harshness, callous attitudes and sometimes ridiculous comments had a lasting impact on the children's psyches. My mother's family's general attitude toward us as children strongly suggests the kind of odds we were battling against from the starting line.

My family hurriedly acquainted themselves with me following a meeting that they'd conveniently convened at my aunt's home in Gary. The family meeting was necessary, in their view, to get better acquainted with me; some of them I was meeting was the first time. There was much general conversation about common things such as the weather, community, and the city. The old patriarch of the family clan was Uncle Moses. There were about three other relatives with him as they comfortably situated themselves in my aunt's living room. After about fifteen to thirty minutes of general conversation, they zeroed in on the family. Uncle Moses had a sister who had taught and had retired from public school in Lexington, Mississippi. She was also married and had a family. Uncle Moses had worked and retired from a vocation of cooking on the Illinois Central Railroad. His sister, Mrs. Jessie Rhymes had, I believe, two daughters and two sons. The youngest boy of the family had attending and graduated from Jackson State University.

Now, after much general conversation Uncle Moses turned the conversation to me. I could hear everything, because the room Aunt Jessie had rented to me was situated just next to her living room. And so, when Uncle Moses asked the question:

"Whose boy is that in that room?" My Aunt Jessie replied: "That is one of Jannie's younger boys, his name is T.J... come on out here, boy, and speak to Uncle Moses. You know he is here from Chicago; he is a big cook on the Illinois Central Railroad."

I quickly responded, "yes, ma'am!"

He asked me a few pointed questions, none of which I thought was significant; they were merely asked to evaluate and size me up as a person, since I was an offspring of the McClellan clan. After the brief interrogation, I quickly dismissed myself and returned to my designated room. That is when they began to talk loudly about my family, and particularly about my father. Uncle Moses compared me to his sister's youngest boy, I believe his name was Telee Rhymes. My aunt had stated loudly that I was a college graduate, and Uncle Moses sarcastically and cynically asked, *what* college?"My aunt asked me the name of the institution I'd graduated from. I proudly stated, "Mississippi Valley State University!" Uncle Moses rhetorically responded, "he will never teach here in Gary, Indiana because he ain't as smart as sister Jessie's boy! You know, Sister Jessie's boy is a graduate of Jackson State College. He is very smart."

Be that as it was, their evaluation of me did not determine my fate nor my reality. Shortly after their interrogation and assessment of my value in their minds, I decided to do some investigating of my own. I asked my Aunt Jessie where the Gary Public Board of Education was located. Reluctantly, she told me where it was located but I never revealed to my aunt why I'd inquired where the Gary Public School District was specifically located. After about a week had passed I decided to make a trip to the Gary Indiana Public Board of Education. The Board of Education was located at 21st Avenue & Virginia. I was working the second shift, 4p.m. to 12 midnight, at Inland Steel Corporation in East Chicago, Illinois. I had to get up early in the morning anyway, because I was paying my Aunt Jessie $32 monthly just to stay with her; I had to provide my daily meals for myself. Occasionally, my aunt would feel convicted by the Holy Spirit and offer me a meal when she came in from church. Whenever she did, she would name a plethora of things she wanted done to her home along the line of 'handy-man' repairs to her home while we were eating. Of course, I would listen engagingly and attentively during the course of our meal, as if I would do the jobs she wanted done. However, as soon as she was done naming the jobs, my response was, "yes, Aunt Jessie, I heard you name the repairs you want me to do to your home. However, Aunt Jessie, I don't do handy man repairs." Then, she would just literally lose it! She would go through countless profanities directed toward me. I jokingly indulged her, allowing her to vent and compare me to my oldest brother who had lived with her many years prior to me—but it didn't matter how much she cursed and bad-mouthed me. I am sure she learned two things about me that were distinctly different from my oldest brother. Firstly, if I said I wasn't going to do something, it didn't matter about the cursing, brow-beating, and excoriating—I wasn't going to do it. Secondly, my aunt learned that I was reliable and dependable.

In the final analysis, an endearing and lasting relationship was formed between us that endures to this day. The thing that was the knockout-punch to my Aunt Jessie and the others in the Pempleton family: contrary to their predictions, I became a public-school teacher at Beckman Jr. High School right before my family's eyes.

CHAPTER SEVEN

When I walked into the Board of Education one Monday morning in late October of 1970 I was introduced to a tall, handsome Black man named Mr. Van Humbrick. Mr. Humbrick was the personnel director for the Gary Public School District. Following our brief introduction and further scrutiny of my credentials, he informed me that he had an immediately opening in my area of Science at Beckman Jr. High School; if I was interested, the position was mine upon my acceptance. Indeed, I was, so immediately I was accepted. He instructed me to take the application to my residence and complete it. Upon my returning the completed application, we would discuss the particulars of the contract and he would retroactively allow for all of the school year, salary-wise.

The lesson I learned from that entire ordeal: even when everything seems meaningless in life, God still has a purpose for our life. I was too carnal to recognize this when my family had rejected me and literally criticized me to the point of ostracism. When it often seems that our lives swing from drudgery to challenges we don't want, I personally ask: God, help me to see You in the midst of whatever faces us; show me a small glimpse of the purpose and meaning You bring to everything.

I prepared to report to Beckman Jr. High School on Grant Street, which was southeast of Roosevelt High School, as I remember. I reported to the junior high school on a Monday morning to meet the principal, Mr. Jasper Sykes. I also met his secretary. During my introduction, I was also introduced to the assistant principal, Mr. Nelson, who gave me a tour of the school. He also showed me my classroom. Over the course of the tour he hadn't officially introduced me to the staff and faculty, so as he took me through the school, I was examined with eyes of curiosity by staff and students.

During the process I was continuously stalked and watched by the principal's secretary, Ms. Evelyn Rhymes. Now, this lady was in her late fifties or mid-sixties, but trust me: with no exaggeration, this sister went all "nilly-willy" crazy whenever she saw me. It was so obvious, you could hear sighs, groans, cat-calls all over the principal's office. Immediately after I got back to my aunt's house I began to tell her how this lady had conducted herself. Well, wouldn't you know! My aunt gave me all the news on Ms. Evelyn Rhymes. As a matter of fact, my Aunt Jessie told me that it was Ms. Rhymes' modus operandi to spend her hours at work trying to catch herself a young strong, capable, available, and handsome brother. Well, that was the beginning of my troubles in Gary, Indiana.

After being officially introduced to the staff and faculty at Beckman J. High School, I met my colleagues. Naturally, being young and footloose and fancy-free, so to speak, I wasn't turning down any young ladies. This is why I can say unequivocally to any young person: if you do not have a standard or criteria for yourself, you are in deep and serious trouble!

Let me preface my statement by declaring that I have been very blessed and favored by God! I say this because at that point in my life I did not pray for permission or forgiveness. However, let me say by way of testimony, that if the Lord allows you to live long enough, your life experiences will bring you to Him or drive you away from Him.

After I accepted my assignment teaching Science, my students took to me immediately. They bonded with me and I bonded with them because they saw immediately that I loved children. They also picked up immediately that I was concerned about them beyond their lessons and how they conducted themselves in the classroom. I always taught students from the affective approach I learned early in my teaching career. I believe it was during my student teaching.

Students really don't care what you know academically until they learn how much you care.

And so, as I settled into my first teaching assignment, there were several young colleagues that caught my eye. Of course, my interest was in the city of Gary, and so, as was my custom, I would work hard during the week and on Friday nights I would come home after a good meal and sleep until about 9:30p.m. or 10:00p.m. Following my usual sleep pattern, I would hit the streets. At 21st and Broadway there was a nightclub called the Blue Note. The Blue Note Night Club was a jazz club approximately five blocks from my aunt's house. I began to visit this club every Friday night about 9:30 or 10:00p.m. after I got up. I was still driving my 1970 Pontiac GTO. It was metallic tan with a cream-colored top. As was my custom, I would come in the club have a drink or two then I would drive to Chicago, which is thirty miles west of Gary. Of course, Chicago had a couple of night clubs I often visited. One was the Burning Spear and the other was Roberts Hotel. Those were the clubs I attended almost every weekend. Rarely did I hang out in Gary; I never was very fond of Gary because to me it was a large, industrial smoke-infested city under constant, lingering clouds of rust and soot that constantly pervaded the atmosphere. The people seemed very cliquish and clannish in their behaviors and mannerisms, always looking for an opportunity to ensnare, entrap, or jam you up. This prevailing mentality exhibited by many of my brothers and sisters in the African American community always baffled and fascinated me in many ways. As I continued to adapt to the culture of the city I began to realize that, even in the educated community, there were varied instances among individuals that were just inherently ignorant. For lack of a better expression, it seemed that some folks waited for the right moment to seize and entrap you, and literally devour you. After adjusting and adapting in that culture, and making some mistakes in the process, I quickly learned that if a person did not have a strong sense of family identity, self-worth, and purpose, he or she would become a prostitute for whatever the world threw at them.

Reflecting on my social and night life in Gary and Chicago, it was customary to start my evening at the Blue Note Jazz Club on 21st and Broadway almost every Friday night. When I encountered an attractive lady in the club, especially if she was unescorted, I would make inquiry from the bartender as to who she was. Of course, I was trying to determine whether she was alone or if she was with some gentleman in the club. Once the bartender gave me the all-clear signal, then I would make my move. Now back in the day, a gentleman would either send a lady a word via the bartender or send her a drink, after inquiring what her drink was. If she accepted the drink, that simply meant the course was clear and you could make your move.

I happened to meet a young lady at the Blue Note by the name of Sherri James. We met, talked, and as per my custom, I later went to Chicago to the Burning Spear or to Roberts Hotel. Since I had siblings residing in Chicago, I would often spend the weekend in Chicago. Many times, I would return to Gary to my aunt's house well after midnight, with just time enough to take a bath and get ready for classroom on Monday morning. This was pretty much my routine while staying with my aunt. One day to my surprise, my aunt started talking to me in codes; she started throwing out hints about my behavior the worse my behavior became. I am sure I didn't take what my aunt was attempting to tell me seriously. I never stopped once to think that, since my aunt had been living in Gary long before I was born, she knew people in Gary that were virtually impossible for me to have known. However, I was young, dumb and full of myself and thought I knew everything. Now that I think about it, one of my favorite brothers-in-law frequently told me that I concentrated my brain where an opossum carried his fat!

Now that I have reached the age where I have an opportunity to write my autobiography, I now know beyond a shadow of a doubt that nothing but God's grace and mercy has sustained me. My prayer is that this book might be a testimony to someone who abides in the residence of despair and oppression; that they might somehow catch a ray of hope and conclude with confidence and conviction: if brother Thomas J. McClellan did it, so can I.

Despite my aunt's hinting, scolding and browbeating, I was determined to continue the path I was on. One rainy Saturday morning I was driving back from a Friday night of partying in Chicago, probably at the Burning Spear or perhaps the popular Robert's Hotel. As I came into Gary at about 2:30 or 3:00a.m. in the morning and exited off the 94 East Expressway heading to Broadway and 25th Avenue, who did I see in the fog and misty rain? To my surprise and astonishment, it was Sherri James, the wife of the captain of Gary's police force! Immediately I stopped my GTO, pulled to the curb and shouted, "hey girl, what are you doing out here?" "Hey Thomas, I have been looking for you!," she replied.

Now mind you, I had no idea at the time she was married. My Aunt Jessie had been warning me, but Auntie's messages to me had been in codes rather than direct. You know how they talked to you back in the day: *'boy, the night has eyes!'*, *'boy, you better be careful, you gonna run into a snag!'* How about this one? *'Boy, you had better be careful, there is a limb in your road.'* You know, all of those sayings. Really, those were just a few. These were the things my Aunt said to me instead of just coming straight to the point. But you know, I love her even more today, because while her affection for her nephew was paradoxical in its expressions, the Creator had my back all the time and was constantly ordering my steps—even while I was dealing with the Gary Police Captain's wife and did not know it. My aunt knew it all along and would not tell me in plain English; but I've heard it said over and over again, "the good Lord takes care of old folks and fools." I am sure I would not be that emphatic and plain-spoken if I did not have evidence to support my claim.

Let's go back to the Saturday morning Sherri stopped me at 25th and Broadway while it was misty raining at 2:30a.m. or 3:00a.m. in the morning. I did notice that after I had allowed her to get into my car, an automobile followed my car down Broadway to 5th Avenue. After we arrived at 5th Avenue, we turned to go to East Chicago, Ill. Now, little did I know that a car was trailing us the entire time since I'd picked her up at 25th and Broadway. However, by me being under the influence of alcohol, I did not become suspicious of us being followed at all. As the story goes, when we arrived in East Chicago, Ill., Sherri got us a hotel room. As we got situated in this flea-bag hotel room, she started demanding that we have sex but as fate would dictate the situation, I told her I was sleepy and insisted that I get some sleep. Perhaps, an hour, to an hour and a half later—about 6:30 or 7:00a.m. Saturday morning—there was a series of rapid knocks on the door along with a forced entrance! Immediately, Captain Wallace James and his deputy stepped in. Sherri started screaming and shouting, "don't kill Thomas! It's not his fault!"

In the meantime, Wallace's deputy had a .357 Magnum pressed to my nose, asking the Captain, "what do you want me to do with this son-of-a-bitch?" All during this time, Sherri was steadily screaming her husband's name and pleading with him to spare my life. She constantly repeated that it was not my fault. About that time, he told his deputy to let me go. However, Wallace then hit his wife with a pair of brass knuckles and cut one of her eyes completely out of the socket. About that time, I was frozen stiff; my mind was completely blank. In a moment's notice, I saw my life flash before my face as if it were a panoramic scene. In a split second my mind went back to Mississippi, and my life reviewed from my childhood and brought me to that present moment in my life. When the deputy took the gun from my nose, I was so disoriented and confused. When I started my car, I had driven to Whiting, Illinois before I finally came to myself. Captain James threw his wife across his shoulder and took her out of the hotel.

One would have thought I had learned my lesson. However, Sherri filed charges against her husband, so I was summoned to court and had to testify. I told the truth. Frankly, I did not know she was married and that they had a son. Shortly after my court appearance and testimony, my car was filled with a substance that locked the engine. My uncles met with me at 19th and Broadway at a breakfast restaurant. There, my Uncle Sandy and Uncle Robert Pempleton told me clearly and plainly that I had to get out of Gary, Indiana. I did not dispute them; quite frankly, I agreed with them wholeheartedly. I told them I was ready to go, but there was just one problem: my motor was locked up in my car, and I had no other source of transportation. Uncle Sandy said to me, "T.J., I have found you a rebuilt engine to go in your car and I have the mechanic to install it for you. I believe he told me the entire job would cost approximately $850.00."

In the meantime, the Gary Public School system was on strike. I had managed to contact the Springfield Public School system and the general superintendent, Mr. Ed Eberhart. Mr. Eberhart had set up an interview with me and after I drove to Springfield, Ohio. Mr. Eberhart employed me at Keifer Jr. High School as head of the Science Department. Mr. Eberhart got me situated in an apartment in a nice neighborhood.

Before I left Gary, I had the opportunity to meet my aunt's family physician, a Panamanian named Dr. DuBois, who had at one time taught in the Gary Public School system. He had taught at Pulaski Middle School, which was located in Gary.

Dr. DuBois was a very warm and personable man. He naturally had a 'gift for gab', so to speak, and he had the uncanny ability to discern talent and ability upon acquaintance. Immediately after my aunt introduced us, he asked me a few pointed questions about science—specifically Biology—to check out my ability and adeptness in the field. I gave him the answers as soon as he asked them. He gave immediate feedback and the confirmation that I had the natural ability for medicine. My Aunt Jessie was so impressed, she could hardly contain herself—and to really affirm his approval and confidence in me, he invited me to work with him, to assist and take me under his wings as my mentor. Of course, after my aunt and I left his office, Satan entered my spirit and started a personal conversation with me. Satan showed me all the negatives in Dr. DuBois. He pointed out to me that that doctor was homosexual and he showed me all the ways that Dr. DuBois would destroy my life. Naturally, considering my past life and my dysfunctional upbringing, I agreed with Satan and that was the end of that opportunity.

In conjunction with these positives things happening to me, I was surrounded by a multitude of negatives. With all due respect and honesty, my lifestyle was not filled with the best of positive affirmations. While I was surrounded by both married and single female colleagues, I chose to start associating myself with this married woman. My aunt had been instrumental in introducing me to this beautiful young Gullah sister from Charleston, South Carolina named Joan Meyers. Joan was a beautiful Black woman who spoke with the Geechee dialect. She was beautifully built; really, she had an hourglass shape. If my memory serves me correctly, she taught Special Education at Beckman Jr. High School. We briefly dated for a while, but Joan was seeing another fella who was a star basketball player for Roosevelt High School in Gary, Indiana. When I see the actress Gabrielle Union, my mind often thinks of Joan Meyers. Frequently, we would have lunch at McDonald's Restaurant. In fact, Joan Meyers was the first lady that introduced me to McDonald's;

when we were working together at Beckman Jr. High School we frequently had our lunch there. Joan was a very intelligent, engaging, and affectionate woman. Although we never had a sexual relationship we were strongly attracted to each other.

My Aunt Jessie had much to do with our meeting each other. Aunt Jessie had heard that I had met a married colleague named G. Cotten. Her husband taught Music at Roosevelt High School. G. Cotten was from Bentonia, a town in the Mississippi delta near Yazoo City. She came from a large family. Her biological family consisted of about five brothers and three sisters, and she was the oldest girl of the family clan. I recall her telling me her husband was named D.C.; she told me he was from Nashville, Tennessee.

G. taught Social Studies at Beckman Jr. High School. She had a very aggressive and dominant nature. Ms. Jones was her best friend. Ms. Jones started dating my home boy J. Joyner, whom we fondly called 'Stack'. J. taught Physical Education at Beckman Jr. High School. When the Gary Public School system went on strike in 1971 Stewart and his wife, and J. and I were fortunate enough to get employment in the Springfield, Ohio Public School system. Before I move forward to discuss our saga in Springfield, let me complete the story in Gary and my acquaintance with G.

My Aunt Jessie was employed in the Gary Public School system as a sanitation worker, and naturally my aunt was privy to all the gossip and negative news about the staff and teachers in the community schools in Gary. Now as I review my teaching experience in Gary, I see that my aunt always had my best interest at heart, regardless of how I conducted myself; after all was said and done, I was her nephew. While I may not have had the knowledge and experience I have now, it doesn't negate the fact that my behavior and conduct did have an impact on the family.

As immature and unlearned as I was, my understanding and knowledge of what really mattered was extremely limited. My value system was centered on me, myself, and I at that moment in my life. I had very little interest in building formidable and spiritual relationships simply because I was the center of my world. Thank God, I've lived long enough to come into the knowledge that it's wrong—whether in business, family, or the house of God—to view others from the perspective of how they can benefit us. I had to live a little while before I stopped valuing people for what I could get from them rather than focusing on how I could serve them in Jesus' name. I have come to accept what Paul talked about in his letter to the Philippians, *"Do nothing out of selfish ambition or vain conceit. Rather in humility value others above yourselves, not looking to your own interests but each of you to the interests of the others."*

I thank God and a few other responsible people for their prayers to aid and assist me in learning that people are not to be used for our own self-aggrandizement and selfish benefit. People are loved by God and I am loved by God therefore we must love one another. I am thankful beyond measure; I have come to learn and accept that God's love is the greatest love in the universe. And so, my constant prayer is: *teach me Lord, to see people as You do. Bearing Your image, being worthy of Your love and needing Your care, may Your great love find in my heart a vessel through which that love can be displayed.*

Thank God I have lived long enough to know joy comes from putting another's needs ahead of your own. After G. and I began seeing each other, she started coming to my aunt's house after school. When I answered the door, she would do things to make me almost lose it. Naturally, my aunt had neighbors watching her home; my aunt remediated the problem by having me to move out of her house to stay with a lady who ran a boys' home in Gary. I don't recall the lady's name. I just know this lady rented me a room and she had about ten boys she was taking care of. I don't know if this lady's home and program was subsidized by the State of

Indiana or if it was a program through the church. I honestly don't remember now.

My move did not stop G. from coming to the lady's house. I vividly remember G. and I had set up a time to play hooky from school together for a sexual encounter at the Holiday Inn. After that encounter, I honestly believe G. thought she owned me! As I said previously, she was an extremely aggressive woman. I had the opportunity to see her husband. He was short in stature and he was a very timid and insecure man.

G. always talked about the fact she wanted a baby boy; she was never fond of girls. When I met her she and her husband had been married a number of years, but I don't recall exactly how long they had been married. Her best friend was J. Glenn.

I don't recall asking why G. and her husband did not have children. She specifically told me her husband said that her womb was tilted, therefore she could not get pregnant. I honestly believe her husband was not virile enough to get her pregnant. Not only was G. extremely aggressive, she was diagnosed as having a manic depressant personality.

As time progressed, I was fortunate to find employment in Springfield, Ohio. Through a procedure called reciprocity, the license bureau of the State Board of Education in Indiana worked in sync with the Board of Education in Ohio. It really simplified the license process for teaching. True to form, I thought that once I got to Springfield I could start anew. Little did I know, I still had to learn the hard way: you cannot outrun your past. My oldest sister Inez McClellan Jones, who is now deceased, used to say to me frequently: "your reputation goes before you and your character is actually who you are when you are alone."

Here I am, seventy-two years age, putting pen to paper to complete my autobiography—a task that I have been planning to do for the last thirty years. G. was a very crafty and wise woman; but quite frankly and honestly, I don't think she ever had an ounce of genuine love for me. I do believe she met a young and confident man from Mississippi and decided over a period of our actions and interactions, 'I am gonna get him.' The reason I say this is based upon her interactions with me during the course of our relationship. She loaned me money to get set up in Springfield, Ohio when I left Gary, Indiana under duress. She said she borrowed the money from her grandmother, and I don't recall the exact amount I borrowed from her. However, because I borrowed the money from her, I do believe she thought she'd purchased me.

While I was in the process of repaying her, she made an unannounced trip to my apartment in Springfield. I had just begun my new teaching assignment at Keifer Jr. High School. I had a female neighbor across the hall and while G. was at my place, that neighbor pretended she wanted to borrow a cooking utensil. Now, that was the first and only time my new neighbor had ever been in my apartment. Of course, she and G. had small talk that really wasn't about anything, in my opinion. However, when it was all over G. hit the ceiling with all kind of brow-beating and negative remarks accusing me of going with her and having a sexual relationship—none of which was true! In retrospect, that was my cue to leave her alone, but I'll just say this to try to help somebody: God will show you the devil many, many times. But if you don't have the sense to recognize him or her, then ultimately, you are on your own.

After G. got the fight started, she ran and got into her Toyota to head back to Gary. Angry and upset, and operating on nothing but testosterone and ego, I cut her off in my car and backed up traffic for miles while we had a public fight. G. had a mysterious and enigmatic nature. She would drive me with whatever it took—even disrespect—until a physical fight ensued; afterwards, she would be satisfied. To this day, I never understood that mystique about her. But then, there were several things I never understood about her.

On a positive note, despite all the negative things that occurred to me in Springfield, Ohio, many good things happened to me as well.

After I had begun my teaching experience there, I met a young Caucasian physician. I guess I must have been teaching in the city about three or four months. We got into a conversation about my major in college and my occupation. I told him I was a teacher at Keifer Jr. High School. Bluntly, he asked if I had ever considered studying medicine. I told him of my encounter with Dr. DuBois in Gary, Indiana. He told me that he would arrange for me to take the medical exam and set up an interview with Mr. Jack Marsh, a pharmaceutical representative recruiter for the Upjohn Company of Kalamazoo, Michigan. The young physician arranged it so that I took the medical exam one Saturday morning at one of the local schools. I reported promptly on Saturday morning to the school and the medical exam started promptly at 8:30a.m. Every part of the examination was sufficiently timed, and at approximately two of three p.m. it was all over. When I got the results back, my overall score ranked me in the 95th percentile. My weakest suit was writing. When the young physician and I talked again, he gave strong words of encouragement and urged me to be a pharmaceutical representative. The doctor sent Mr. Marsh to my apartment in Springfield one Saturday morning, and he stayed all day. As I reflect on the experience, Mr. Marsh behaved as if he was sent on a specific mission. He knew the exact specifications of the African American male he was looking for because he had been given the criteria from the district manager of Upjohn Company.

Contrary to my belief and my behavior, I believe I was born with a genetic predisposition in my DNA to be above average. Although there were certain mitigating circumstances in my environment during my early childhood that were very stifling to my early childhood schooling and academic

119

preparation, I know from first-hand experience, deprivation does not validate ignorance.

Now that I have reached this place in my life, I certainly find peace in the stillness of my soul. As I reflect back over my life, in my quest to live a fulfilling life, I may have looked and sought contentment from a variety of sources. People, places, or things may bring temporary satisfaction, but thank God, I am at a place where my heart yearns for something greater. Once upon a time, I may have wandered off the spiritual path of understanding and yes, I did indeed reside in the congregation of the dead. I have since learned to drink from the presence of God and continually discipline and train my mind to stay focused on a spirit-led path. Throughout the day, I pause to empty my mind of negative stress and to invite God's spirit to fill my heart. As I daily practice and nurture this mindset, I find the lasting satisfaction of inner peace in the stillness of my soul.

And so, at the end of that Saturday when Mr. Jack Marsh completed his thorough examination, I was employed by the family-owned business, the Upjohn Medical and Pharmaceutical Company of Kalamazoo, Michigan. I recalled calling my mother and sharing the exciting and grand news that the Upjohn Company had chosen me to be a salesman for them. My mother did not like the idea at all; she had no problems in letting me know I should have stayed in the teaching profession and public-school system.

Being that I have always been the type of person I am, regardless of my mother's guidance, prayers and instructions, I had to find my own limitations on this journey called life. One of the things I'm most grateful for is that while others doubted, threw stones of scorn, and shot arrows of despair and castigation, my mother never left my side; even in my darkest hours.

I am certain without any doubts or equivocations, the worst thing I did was to continue dealing with Mrs. G. Cotten. After one of the worst fights with a female I'd ever had in my entire life, she was somehow cunning and clever enough to get back into my good grace by convincing me it was all *my* fault. Now that I look back over my life and reflect on the ways and nuances of our relationship, it had no recourse to end, except the way it did end—if for no other reason than that it was not built on genuine spiritual divine love. She did not have any genuine love for me. I would venture to say, for the benefit of both of us, the entire relationship was built on lust.

To be totally transparent and honest, G. J. M. Cotten never really knew Thomas James McClellan. We were both thirty-one years of age, but truthfully speaking, neither one of us really knew each other. There were things I never knew about G. until I married her in May 1975 at her grandmother's house at 8509 So. Morgan St., Chicago, Ill. I never knew G. had a severe chemical imbalance until I married her. Although our first child was lost to miscarriage, Kelly, our son was born September 13, 1973. When I went to work for the Upjohn Company, G. and I were still seeing each other. There is a movie called "Play Misty For Me" starring Clint Eastwood. As I reflect over the entire episode my mind frequently goes back to that movie, because it is the best thing in art form that gives a true illustration of our entire relationship.

I can honestly say, there are some people that are naturally toxic for your life. With honesty and due respect, I felt from the day I married G. that it was never genuine love. Every marriage is not built on love, respect, and mutuality. I recall taking G. to meet my oldest sister, who then resided at 4844 So. State Street, which was the Robert Taylor's projects. At that time my sister and her husband were living on the 18th floor. When I introduced G. to my sister and her family, I will never forget the sarcastic and cynical smirk G. had on her face! Some days later, my sister and I talked, and I asked her assessment of G.

"Boy, you ain't got yourself shit, but you don't know that," was my oldest sister's response, "but if you married her, you'll find out."

I did not heed my sister's advice, because G. was the mother of my only son. To be totally honest, I did love her. Oh, I remember after that encounter that I did allow G. to talk to my mother by telephone. When my mother and G. were done talking, my mother advised me to get away from her as soon as I could. There were even people in the Upjohn Company such as my district manager, Richard Dudex and others, who advised me against marrying her. Still, I was determined to marry her.

While I sold medicine for the Upjohn Company, my territory consisted of approximately one hundred-fifty medical doctors with varying specialties. There were approximately two hundred-fifty pharmacies and approximately five hospitals. My territory was largely the inner city of Cleveland, Ohio. Consequently, my territory consisted of a large percentage of African American physicians. Many of them were impressed with my knowledge of science as well as my knowledge of medicine. At that time, the federal government had mandated that the pharmaceutical companies in this country employ a certain percentage of African American representatives. With that being the case in the early 70s, pharmaceutical houses around America started considering the best minds that they could find in the African American community. Several times after being considered for the job, Caucasians approached me with the notion that my last name was McClellan, therefore I was not an African American. However, as you might imagine, it did not take me long to get them straight on that nonsense. I referred to the concept of miscegenation and how it was exploited in the transport of the slave ships from Africa; it did not take very long to put that argument to rest for once and always.

I was frequently challenged with the opportunity to study medicine. On numerous occasions, physicians—both

Caucasian and African American—discussed with me the possibility of me going on to medical school. I would always come up with some kind manufactured excuse, premeditatedly or spontaneously. One day I was challenged by Dr. E.J. McCampbell, this nice African American physician who had his own clinic in East Cleveland, Ohio on Kinsman Avenue. He was a graduate of Howard University Medical School and was also a trustee. He challenged me one day as he and I were talking. As was my routine on many Friday evenings, I stopped by his office for my final call for the week. He and I had a very good platonic relationship. He asked me point blank, "McClellan, I'm a trustee; if you're serious about medicine, I can get you into Howard. What's really the hold up?" I made up my mind to come straight with him, because he was truly a friend and sincerely had my best interest at heart. I confessed to him that I had a son by G. He told me that I could be of much greater help to him with a medical degree rather than as a pharmaceutical representative. As he pressed me in the conversation he concluded the verbal exchange by saying, "why don't you bring the young lady to Cleveland so I can meet her?" I agreed to do that and took G. to his office to meet him. Dr. McCampbell met her and he had a brief conversation with her. Following his conversation with her, he bluntly told me, "you will never go to medical school."

As I reflect on that moment and that statement made by Dr. McCampbell, it was obvious that he knew many things I didn't. At the time we met, he was old enough to be my father. He knew that I was intelligent enough to go to medical school; however, he could assess my core values by evaluating my associates—specifically, the type of woman I had chosen to be the mother of our child. Raw knowledge and book preparation may have manifested in my mannerisms and our conversations; but as he critiqued me as a total person, he immediately recognized major character flaws. I showed low aim, poor judgment in selecting a female companion, and lack of self-confidence. Dr. McCampbell knew I had the mental ability, however there were some other major components missing in my character and personality that were essential in achieving my goal as a physician.

Now that I have had time to not only think about the missed opportunity but to put all the pieces of the puzzle in place, I have come to that place where I am comfortable with everything I have seen, heard, eaten, smelled, been told, and forgotten. It is all of these things that make us, and that is why I now try to make sure that my experiences are positive. I am at a place where I can say with conviction: I have encountered many defeats, but ultimately I am not defeated.

CHAPTER EIGHT

Against all the advice from my family and colleagues with the Upjohn Company, G. and I got married May 3, 1975. Early in the morning before leaving Cleveland to get married to her, I vividly recall the Holy Spirit awakening me with a swift kick in my back. I jump straight up from my bed. A voice said to me in plain English: *"do not marry her!"* But as clearly as I had heard the voice, I blatantly and vigorously disobeyed it.

I confess openly and under any set of circumstances, my life was a living hell while G. and I were married, from May 3 1975 to April 1976. She was still teaching in Gary. Now that I think about it again, I also went against the advice of my mother. My mother strongly advised me to bring all of my extra household items to Mississippi rather than take them to Chicago to G's family. Again, I was disobedient; I took all of my household accumulations to G's family. Now mind you, G. and I had established our own home in Cleveland. G. was pregnant with our second child when we got married May 3, 1975; she'd had a miscarriage and lost our daughter shortly after we were married. Even during this turbulent and challenging transition, the Upjohn Company and my district manager, Mr. Richard Dudex stood by my family and me.

G. had several episodes of illness shortly after we were married. Her ultimate objective was to get us back to Chicago with her people. Frankly, had G. been honest and transparent about the entire marriage, we'd have never been married. Truthfully speaking, G. had never truly and honestly wanted to marry me. Now that I have had a lot of time to honestly assess and evaluate the nuances and particulars of our marriage, I feel that G.'s heart was never committed to a marriage with me. Now I know love is blissful and blinding. Too many people—family, acquaintances, co-workers, and others—told me so! But even as flawed as I am in character, I truly wanted to be a husband, father and provider.

G. came from a matriarchal family. I believe there were about five brothers and three sisters in their biological family. She told me her mother had been a public school teacher, and that she had transitioned this life from a rare blood disease. Mrs. R., whom G. fondly called Granny, was the head of their family clan. I don't recall exactly when the family relocated from Bentonia, Mississippi to Chicago.

I mention the family structure to lead into my next major point that perhaps will shed major light on G.'s disposition and character: I learned she was the victim of a serious chemical imbalance. Clinically speaking, she had been diagnosed as manic depressive. Now mind you, none of this had been said to me or mentioned during the course of our courtship or relationship. Consequently, after I had moved all of our household accumulations to Chicago with her people, that is when I began to see G. for who she truly was.

Her family, and particularly her grandmother, was supportive of our marriage and its success. There I was: torn out of a job I loved; married for the first time; both public school teachers, and both thirty-one years of age—fully matured adults working in our chosen professions. As turbulent and tumultuous as our marriage was, G. initiated counseling with her therapist, a psychiatrist who had been seeing her over the years. His name was Dr. Wiggatow. There were several scheduled sessions with him, sometimes with both of us. There were times when we were scheduled to see him separately. I recall a time I was scheduled to see him alone.

At that particular visit, he asked me to describe my biological family structure. I told him I came from a patriarchal family and described to him the relationship between my father and I. Upon further investigation he discovered the relationship between my father and I was turbulent, chaotic, and dysfunctional. The doctor had me to do some 'role play' episodes. As he proceeded with the analysis, he asked me which of my siblings I grew up with, since we were born in different time intervals. I told him that I mostly identified with my younger sister and the youngest boy in the family. Before I had given him a description of my family structure, he told me the following information regarding my marital situation with G. and her family: "Thomas, you will never have a peaceful and successful marriage with G., simply because you both came from two different family structures." I then asked him to state things plainly and be straightforward, because it was necessary and essential to my survival as a man and human being. He responded, since I requested that kind of explanation, he would tell me point blank: "Thomas, you came from a patriarchal family with a strong father as head of your family. G. did not come from that type of structured family. She came from a family where women ruled." In other words, she came from a matriarchal family structure. He then said to me, "she will kill you before she will submit to you. You need to get away from her and her family as soon as you can. In fact, you need to go back to Mississippi and connect with the siblings you grew up with. And when you do, make sure it is around plenty of water."

"What will they do to Kelly, my son?," I quickly asked.

"Nothing. It is you they want to destroy; and Thomas, they will kill you," he warned.

Following this startling revelation, I repeated my pointed question concerning our son Kelly T. McClellan:

"What will they do to him?"

"Nothing," he assured me without hesitation or reservation. "They want *you* out of the picture; in fact, G. wants you dead."

I can tell you without a doubt: that was a moment of truth Dr. Wiggatow revealed to me. I didn't hesitate and I didn't minimize the information the good doctor had given me. The information the doctor gave me was as if God was speaking through him.

I did not say a word to G. nor her family about the information the doctor had shared with me. To be totally honest, I was dealing with my own issues. It was the first time I had been married, and we were also marrying into a ready-made family that we had created. I confess, I loved G. and Kelly with all my heart and all my strength, as you might imagine. However, as honest and transparent as my confession is, G.'s attitude and disposition were convoluted. She was enigmatic. I am sure of that. In her own way, she loved Kelly and me. With her illness and the major transition of adjusting to life with her and her family, the process was quite overwhelming to say the least!

Nevertheless, her grandmother Mrs. L. R. and the other family members accepted me, for the most part. But again, I had my own issues. I could never see or imagine myself permitting a woman to be the breadwinner in my family. G. knew I had serious issues with that particular mindset. During our transitioning and adjusting period—if there really ever was one—G.'s tongue could be caustic and super-critical.

One time, my sister had gotten me a job in downtown Chicago. This job consisted of me going to different locations designated by the Health Department of the City of Chicago and working with team members, taking blood pressures in the local community. I recalled specifically getting off work tired and hungry. When I arrived home G. and her sisters and brothers had eaten all the dinner. She had the habit of getting with her sisters and brothers and openly poking fun at my posture. She had the audacity to tell me in the presence of her sisters and brothers, "if your family doesn't want you, you know we don't want you here!" I learned firsthand what Jesus Christ experienced when he was castigated and rejected by his biological family and his church family as well. What G. had in mind, I believe, was to taunt and aggravate me to make me do something destructive to myself—providing her methods and remedies

128

were not working fast enough. I remember the three statements G. said to me during the ceremony on the day I married her, May 3, 1975. One: "I got you, and I am going to fuck you up"; two, "I have got two kids to take care of, Tom and Kelly"; and three: "I know you love me, but that doesn't mean I love you like you love me!"

The final statement was made to me one morning as she was getting ready to go to work at Westside High School in Gary. I asked her to repeat what she had said to me, and she said the exact words again. I asked her again to repeat her words to make sure she heard what she'd said to me! We had rented an apartment from one of their neighbors down the street from the family's home at 8509 So. Morgan Street on the south side of Chicago. After she had left for work in Gary, I decided to gather up as much of my belongings as I could and call a taxi cab to go to my sister's house at 8433 So. Hermitage. Before I left the neighborhood I decided to visited Mrs. L. R.'s home on Morgan. Of course, after I rang the doorbell the old turban-wearing grandmother, Mrs. R. answered the door with half-hearted eye contact and a sheepish grin, saying "come on in, Tom, you look kinda upset this morning."

"Yes ma'am, Mrs. R., I am," I responded.

"What is wrong, Tom? Now you know you and G. can work things out. You all got Kelly, you know."

"Yes ma'am, I know," I told her. "But I am afraid I am going have to go and work on me."

She had in her possession a large, over-sized black purse. Immediately, she opened that purse; to my amazement it was stuffed with money—to be specific, five-dollar bills, ten-dollar bills, twenty-dollar bills, fifty-dollar bills, and hundred-dollar bills.

"This house and the property is already you and G.'s," she told me. "Tom, I've got this for you now—and just know, I have got plenty more where this came from."

I listened to her carefully and critically,

"Yes I know, Mrs. R., but I don't need any of that. I need to go and work on myself!," I said.

"What about your boy, Kelly?," she responded, in a commanding voice.

"You all will take care of him. It is *me* you don't want around here," I responded.

I watched her reaction to what I said, because I'd spoken a truth. Mrs. R. was very shocked with my response to her proposition. After we finished that brief, pointed conversation, we were only in each other's presence two other times prior to her making her transition. I recall seeing her briefly two other times. Once was when my friend and high school classmate John W. Boyette had visited his oldest sister, who resides in Chicago. After John's visit I decided to return to Louisville, Kentucky with him; but before we left Chicago I joined two of my sisters and my oldest brother and we all went to see my son Kelly, who was staying at Mrs. Reese's home. I believe I saw her for the last time around 1982, when my current wife's cousin passed. G. had been saying to me repeatedly, "Tom, Granny wants to see you! You had better hurry." When my wife JoAnn's cousin passed abruptly. I said to her, "why don't we go by to see Mrs. L.R.? After all, we are going to your cousin's funeral."

We went by Mrs. R.'s home. It was the first time JoAnn had seen her, and it was the last time I would see her alive. I recall that evening as if it was yesterday. As JoAnn and I entered the home, she invited us in. She made very brief and kind remarks about JoAnn and then she focused her attention on me. She said, "Tom, I just wanted to see you! Oh, you look so well!"

I was receptive to her kind remark, and as I was exiting the door, I bid her farewell and JoAnn and I were on our way. That was the last time I saw her alive. I have frequently wondered why she wanted to see me; then I reconciled the matter by saying to myself, she never forgot me because I was the first man she encountered that refused her home, land, and money. I discerned the look and the message beyond the expression on her face; she learned from me, by way of principles and character, that all African American men are not swayed by an African American woman's money. Frankly, I don't know whether I startled Mrs. Reese or put her in a state of shock by refusing to take her money. Whatever the case, I can say without a doubt that I'd reached the turning point in my life; I literally could take no more.

By God's grace and mercy, He had orchestrated and directed every step of the saga with G. as my wife. I am certain, God had been in the equation from the first time we met each other. Regardless of what her intentions were initially, God took the entire experience and worked it for my good. There is no way I could write a book and remember with precision how I was treated and mistreated by G. and her family had God not intended it to be. I confess my frailties and shortcomings as well. However, I can honestly say the good Lord brought me to and through the entire experience.

I have come to a place in my life where I have accepted that we learn and grow on this spiritual journey called Life. You know, it is kind of like packing a backpack for a marathon. We must choose to pack only the necessities. And so I have learned to travel light by releasing mental baggage and beliefs that no longer benefit me. I have learned to release agendas, rid myself of unnecessary baggage and trust my inner wisdom. I am open and receptive, and trusting that it is leading me to the highest expression of my spiritual nature. My spiritual journey provides me with opportunities I need to learn and grow. Some steps along my journey will be filled with grandeur while others may feel like walking through a barren desert; however, the longer I travel the more connected I feel to my power source and to everyone I encounter along my path. My destination is an inner kingdom by way of peace, love, and compassion. When I reached a place in my struggle where I was wrestling with a monster much greater than I that would ultimately destroy me, I had no recourse but to let go.

I recalled vividly, when I was in the midst of my marriage dilemma I sought my best friend and oldest brother, Mr. Eddie B. McClellan. At the time my brother was not in the church and had not given his life to Jesus Christ. He and I were together one Saturday afternoon, sitting in his car at 187th& Morgan in Chicago. He point-blank asked me if I wanted any liquor. My answer was 'no!' Now mind you, he had a half-pint of choice alcohol in his car; in fact, he offered me the bottle. I immediately refused the bottle and glass. The next question he asked me was if I wanted a female. My answer was still an emphatic no. He then said these words to me; I don't know where they came from: "Right now T.J., your feet are off the ground." Holding his right hand before my face where I could clearly see his fingers, he supported his right hand with his left hand.

"You are up off the ground now as if someone has you suspended in the air, lifting your entire body in mid-air," he said. "One day T.J., you are gonna get your feet back on the ground; and when your feet get back on the ground, no one will ever get them off again!"

After he had thoroughly ruled out what he knew I loved—women—he then spoke and prophesied about my marriage to G. He could not have spoken a greater truth about my predicament at that specific time, even in spite of all the encouraging words and supportive strategies given me by my oldest sister and brother. This was an ordeal that I had to encounter. My oldest brother is deceased now. He departed this life on Saturday morning, February 21, 2015 at approximately 10:22a.m.

As loving, gracious, and long-suffering as God is in His divine wisdom, power, and glory, this challenge was designed by God to teach me an indelible and lasting lesson for the rest of my days on this earth. And so in the constructing of my autobiography, I just pray and hope it will help to assure someone else that He is a deliverer. It is even more gratifying, uplifting, and reassuring to know God found Gideon in a hole, Joseph in a prison, Daniel in a lion's den. As finite as I am in all of my frailties and shortcomings, there are times I felt unqualified to be used by God; but when I remember, it is an integral portion of God's character to recruit from the pit, and not from the pedestal.

Yes, He allowed G. and I to be married to teach us both a lesson, especially when the central motivation was callous, mundane, and all about the flesh. Even as clear as He made it to me not to marry her, as disparate as we were in character and values, God allowed it to be, to teach me a lesson for the rest of my days on earth.

During our separation, I lived with my oldest sister for a short time at 8433 So. Hermitage in Chicago. My sister was employed by the courts of the City of Chicago. She had connections and powerful influence with the judiciary of the City of Chicago. I remember specifically one Friday afternoon; as was G.'s custom, she came to my sister's house dressed in her Daisy Dukes shorts and showed her natural ass in clowning and disruptive behavior. My sister did everything she could to get me to knock the hell out of her! She said to me several times, "I've got your back, T.J." She meant that the 'boys in blue' in the Chicago Police Department were at her command. Truthfully speaking, my sister had that kind of power and authority with the court system in Chicago during the time G. and I were in the midst of our marital problems. Our marriage ultimately ended in divorce, at the expense of the courts. I did not attack G. physically, because I don't believe in physically attacking women. G. had begun to exhibit behaviors and mannerisms I had never seen in her before. While others had speculated and even drawn foregone conclusions about her character and disposition, these manifestations of her character were totally foreign to me. These attributes had been carefully and deliberately hidden from me for a reason. Now to be totally honest, a few people in my circle of acquaintances and family had already discovered these traits about her. My mother, who had talked to her once by telephone had told me to get away from her. What perplexed me then was how my mother could have stated facts about G., whom she had never seen physically. Of course, that was how simple and naïve I was at that point in my life. During this stage in my life, God had me at the right place to show me who G. really was, and also to deliver me from the wretchedness and diabolical character of who she truly was.

There are no questions or doubts in my mind at all. G. seemed to have one focus and one purpose in her mind, and that was to totally annihilate me. In retrospect, I know she would probably disagree with my assessment of the saga between us, and that's okay; but at the place I am in my life now, I am certain that G. J. M. Cotten McClellan had a plan to get rid of the Rev. Thomas J. McClellan. Mind you, I don't have all the details of her diabolical plan; but I can state unequivocally and emphatically, she had a plan. Fortunately, God had other plans for my life. I say that affirmatively, because there is no other way I could have survived that ordeal if God had not been with me. God even provided a way for me to leave Chicago April, 1976.

CHAPTER NINE

By way of my high school best friend, Mr. John W. Boyette, I left Chicago in late May of 1976; John took me to his home in Louisville, Kentucky and we stayed there for at least two weeks. At that particular time, he too was going through a separation and divorce with his wife. After thoroughly evaluating my friend's situation, I decided that I needed to go to my parents' home. After much discussion and deliberation over our situations, I finally convinced my friend John to drive me to my parents' home in Durant, Mississippi. We left Louisville, Kentucky early Saturday morning. At about 1:00p.m., we were at my parents' residence. I remember the experience as if it were yesterday.

The news had reached my parents that I had nearly lost my mind; and so with that kind of news preceding me to my parents, one can readily imagine the state of mind they were in. Let me say wholeheartedly, that despite the frightening stories that had been spread about me, my mother knew that I would never do any harm to them. There was an old lady assisting with housework in my parents' home when John and I arrived there. Naturally, my parents were concerned and nervous. The old lady who was accompanying my mother started to speak to me in a very gross and deep voice. As I approached and embraced my mother with tears of joy and exuberance, the old lady continued to follow me, speaking in a deep and guttural tone. As I embraced my mother and assured her that it was never my intention to harm them in any shape, form or fashion, my father ran to the back yard and braced himself in a defensive position. Then he began to direct me, "stand up straight, son!" However, he did not permit me to embrace him as I had my mother. My father began to lecture me, while my mother was steadily saying to the family and everyone listening that she did not believe a word that had been said about my state of mind. Despite my broken heart, I saw that my mother never

135

believed I'd do anything to harm her nor any of my siblings. My father continued his lecture, saying, "Son, you did not have your wife." After saying so many things to me, he said, "in my hand I have a black King James Translation of the Bible. Take the bible, and read it from cover to cover. When you see your wife, you will know your wife!"

Then my father said, "your brother and your sister will be here shortly from Moss Point, Mississippi to get you."

True to form, at about 3:30p.m. my youngest sister and youngest brother of the family arrived to pick me up, as my father had said. Just as the psychiatrist had advised, they took me to Moss Point and Pascagoula, Mississippi. These cities are on the Gulf coast of Mississippi. Arriving in Moss Point in my condition was not any fun, to say the least. I can honestly say I was not in the best of mental health. With my youngest sister, Mrs. Lena McClellan-Strange-Seymour, having just recently gotten married, I am certain that my health condition did not contribute to the health of their marriage in a positive way. Upon observation, I appeared physically to be a healthy and robust man; but most of my issues were mental and therefore manifested themselves in many different ways. My sister and my youngest brother decided I should stay with him and his wife and family. I am sure I was a burden to their families; but truthfully speaking, I was a very sick man emotionally and mentally.

My stay with my youngest brother was not very pleasant and peaceful at all. My brother's wife, Mrs. R. D. Gadson-McClellan, was very nice to me. At the time, they had two young boys. Sometimes, they would annoy me, but never anything beyond the normal curiosity of inquisitive children. As time passed, my brother's patience and tolerance came to a squeaking and abrupt halt. Now that I have had many years to honestly reflect on the matter, given the state of my mental health, I know that the strain on both my sister's and brother's marriages wreaked havoc. Strange and bizarre ideas ran through my brother's head concerning his wife and

136

me, which I can honestly say were never true. As sick as I was at the time, it never even entered my mind to do anything to or with my brother's wife.

I have to give my youngest sister accolades and kudos. She wasted no time in connecting with the health community about my condition. Immediately, she got me hooked up with the Singing River Hospital Health Care community. The psychiatrist that starting treating me immediately was Dr. William Bridges. His psychologist was Dr. Lancaster. This team of health care officials wasted no time in evaluating and making a clinical diagnosis of my overall condition. Dr. Bridges and Dr. Lancaster were very adamant about their findings and started me on a regimen of therapy to practice and follow on a daily routine. Almost six months after I began therapy, they had taken me off the medications I was on when I initially met them. One of the things they immediately saw was my lack of interest in myself. One of the things Dr. Bridges emphasized to me that I will remember the rest of my remaining days on this planet is this: the importance of self-actualization. He said, "Thomas, never neglect yourself. Why would you make everyone a priority in your life and you constantly remain an option in theirs?"

My sister and brother saw me go through changes in my life that I would not wish upon my worst enemy. But nonetheless, by God's grace, mercy and divine providence, I have lived to pen my story in my autobiography. My brother took me to a place called "the Village", the red-light district for the cities of both Moss Point and Pascagoula. The Village was a place where men gathered from the neighboring cities and towns to have all types of sexual acts with prostitutes, both male and female. When my brother took me there and put me out of his car, I did not know anyone. Try, if you can, to get a mental picture of the scenario: there I was in a place of hookers, pimps, cutthroats, and low-life people who didn't value life at all. However, as fate would have it, I wandered and walked to a lighted place that was a dining hall and hotel combined. As I walked into the dining hall, a man by the name of Joe MacArthur called me by my brother's name. My brother, William McClellan, was nicknamed Joe also. This man, Joe MacArthur, thought I was my brother! Of course, when he shouted out my brother's name to me I began to tremble and I became visibly nervous. Immediately, he rushed to me and put his arms around me. He began to tell me how he knew my brother 'Big Joe' and as Mr. MacArthur told me how he and my brother had already discussed me, Mr. MacArthur told me the dining hall and hotel belong to him. He told me to go and have breakfast on him, and he also gave me a hotel room—all because of the friendship between him and my brother.

At that time, I had no employment. Mr. MacArthur took me at my word, and he put food in my stomach and a roof over my head, after my youngest brother had put me in a place where I knew no one! And so I began my stay in the Village, renting from Mr. MacArthur during my tenure in the Moss Point and Pascagoula area until my current wife Joann and I were married on June 11, 1978.

I can say by way of testimony, I met and dealt with some of the best people in Moss Point and Pascagoula when I lived in the Village. When my youngest sister found out I was living there, she immediately disapproved of it. When I was there, I made friends with all types of people. They quickly noticed that I was different. Many of them noticed I had been to school, and so on many occasions I used to write letters for them; many of them became my friends. Many of the ladies, both white and Black did sexual favors for me just because of my appearance and conversation. I remember my sister saving my life from a stupid and foolish act. There was a physician that practiced medicine in Moss Point named Dr. Morris. He had a receptionist that worked for him whose name was Bettye Rose. The V.F.W. Club was a part of the crowd that visited the Village, especially on weekends. While

I was employed at Ingall's Shipbuilders, also known as 'the shipyard', I met a young Caucasian male who sold me a .45 army pistol for $100 cash. I meditated and thought on destroying my first wife and her family. Really, that is why I had purchased the .45 army pistol from the white man. As I made up my mind to go to the bus station and purchase a ticket to Chicago, it just so happened that I decided to go to the V.F.W. Club. Unbeknownst to me, Bettye Rose was there that night. She heard me discussing my plans to go to Chicago and kill the entire family. She rushed out of the V.F.W. and called my youngest sister; she told her what she'd heard me telling another person in the club. Now, I'd had no idea that Bettye Rose was at the V.F.W. Club. That Saturday morning around the break of day, someone rang my doorbell. I got up and answered the door, and who did I find standing there but my youngest sister! She then told me word for word what Bettye Rose had overheard me discussing with another person. When my sister was done talking to me and telling me the devastating effects such a stupid idea and heinous crime would have on our family, my heart had changed. I even wonder today if she knows the impact she had on my life, getting my attention and influencing me to change my mind. I experienced many good times during my stay on the Gulf Coast in general, but my youngest sister caught me at a moment in my life that left an indelible impression on me for the rest of my days.

Many interesting things happened to me during my stay on the Gulf Coast before I met and married my current wife. I recalled vividly seeing a man killed in cold blood. His pimp name was "Long Horn". One Saturday morning, an argument ensued between him and Joe MacArthur's brother. Mr. MacArthur's brother was named "Pluto", and both of these men were pimps. They had their whores. For some reason, which I will never know, as the argument between the two men intensified, Mr. Pluto pulled out his gun and shot Mr. Longhorn in the forehead; it seemed as though it took Mr.

Longhorn's body forever to reach the ground. I recalled Mr. Longhorn speaking fondly of me and my work ethic. He used to remark often of me, "no matter what happens in the village, that man is going to work!" I had heard him say to others around him that I resembled the late blues singer, Tyrone Davis. He was from Leland, Mississippi, yet he frequently claimed Chicago as his home.

While I lived on the Gulf Coast, I had several jobs. However, the last job I had before Joann and I left the area August 29, 1979 and relocated to Detroit, Michigan was as a Junior Chemist for First Chemical Corporation. There were only two African Americans employed by the company and when they laid the two of us off, I knew they were not going to call us back. Mr. Jimmy Carter was this nation's reigning president. The south was never satisfied with his governing strategies and techniques. Mr. Ronald Reagan followed Mr. Jimmy Carter, and the south seemed pleased and gratified with Reagan's governing strategies and techniques. In my opinion and assessment of his presidency, he did much to set African American progress back millions of years. Now that I have had all of these years to reflect on my life, I see that the Village community was organized and created economically and politically for the wealthy and elite people of Jackson County. The Village was set in the midst of a low income housing project. The entire economic and political atmosphere of the Village was structured to exploit and utilize African Americans as property and commodities for goods and services. Wealthy and financially sound people had the desire and wealth to use the oppressed, the poor, and the less fortunate as tools for their own personal pleasures. As such, the Village had a certain hierarchical structure. Mr. A.D. McCune was the bail bondsman for the entire Village community. There were other men: Mr. MacArthur, Mr. Collier, and a few others who were allowed to have juke joints and cafes. The V.F.W. club was at the far end of the Village community. It may have been alright to come in as a stranger, but you had better not take too long learning the hierarchy and flow of things. The sooner you learned the Village's system and the structural layout of how things operated and how the women played, the greater your chances to fit in and survive. Given my condition and circumstances at that time, I really can say nothing except hallelujah! With what I witnessed and the experiences I encountered, I have no recourse except to say 'thank you, Lord!' that I survived. I know beyond any testimony and confession, God has truly kept and preserved me well.

I recall precisely, I was walking home from the Ingall's ship yard, musing and meditating on the blessings God had bestowed upon me and my wife. We'd left Pascagoula after having put our furniture in storage, and we'd recently purchased a new 1979 burgundy and cream-colored Chrysler Cordoba, which my wife had selected at the dealership in Pascagoula. We left Pascagoula about mid-August and went to our hometown of Durant. We stayed there, then went to Memphis to spend a night with her brother. Floyd and I got together and changed the oil in our car; however, I did not check behind him. After getting to Detroit, I discovered the oil cap had been left off the engine head where the oil was put in our car. I made that discovery shortly after arriving in Detroit. I can tell you, by leaving the oil cap off it affected the engine performance then, and in the days to come. I chose not to believe it was done intentionally.

We arrived in Detroit on August 29, 1979 at about 3:00p.m. on a Saturday afternoon. We attempted to stay with my sister and her family at 19380 Plainview in Detroit. My sister, Mrs. Lyneva [McClellan] Gipson and her husband Mr. James Gipson had two daughters, Jacqueline and Karen. Lynn and James accepted us with open arms; however, their daughters were adults and of course, coming into a family with their own norms naturally stressed the family a bit. As time progressed, naturally the tension built and the stress of adjustment tightened on all the family members—but cooperative efforts from all willing parties helped us to adjust.

Adapting to the culture of Michigan and adjusting to my sister's and brother-in-law's family values were quite challenging, to say the least. When we arrived in Detroit our car was beautiful and brand new. My wife and I had only been married just a bit more than a year. She and I pulled together, because that's all we knew; and truly, all we had was each other. As fate would have it, my wife and I found jobs shortly after arriving there. Unfortunately, that created jealousy and animosity within my family. My sister's oldest daughter Karen was attending the University of Michigan, and had gotten to her senior year. She met a young man named Warren, and shortly after they started dating he got her pregnant. Of course, after she became pregnant they were married; and naturally, with him not being able to find shelter for Karen and his baby, he moved in Karen's parents' home.

I would have to admit Warren's general disposition and attitude left much to be desired—especially with him attending the University of Michigan. He was abrasive, callous, cynical, insolent, imposing, and very inconsiderate to others, especially once he knew they were from the south; *especially* Mississippi. Several times during the course of a conversation, he was boldly aggressive in pointing out his assumed superiority in intellect and educational preparation. He had no idea how belligerent and intrusive he appeared to be. He was so overbearing and erratic that one day his mannerisms reached a breaking point with me. We actually had a physical confrontation where I cracked him across his head with a short, strong stick of wood; he came to himself after that. My brother-in-law really prevented me from killing him; but as you might imagine, following that encounter we were asked to leave my sister's family's home.

We then moved in with my wife's sister and her husband. My wife and I had already secured employment before leaving my family's home. Joann was employed at a shoe store at Northland Mall. We decided to attend our first church in Detroit as a result of Joann getting her hair done, which was a habit of hers since our marriage. When we discussed finding her a beautician we decided to go into the inncr city of Detroit in search of a beauty parlor for her. We were fortunate enough to find a beauty shop in the inner city of Detroit, specifically, the Linwood area. I don't recall the shop's name, nor do I recall the beautician's name. I just know that following the dressing of my wife's hair, the lady invited us to visit her church. Now mind you, we had been openly encouraged to hurry and come to Detroit by both of our families; however, after accepting their invitations and arriving there, many promises were broken. Our families saw our new car, clothes, and other material possessions and jealousy, envy, and other emotions took over, making it difficult—and in some instances, almost impossible—to adjust to the city. Some of our relatives openly told me we would not make it in Detroit, but we did not allow the negatives to drive us away. The more negatives they fed us, the more we pulled together and stayed on our knees praying.

The first church we attended in Detroit was Greater St. Mark M.B. Church. It was located on Grand River & Ohio, and the Pastor's name was Rev. E.D. Kirby from Roanoke, Virginia. The moment my wife and I entered the church he told the ushers to bring the preacher to the pulpit. Rev. Kirby's assistant Pastor was named Rev. Randolph. Rev. Kirby was indeed a living prophet. When I refused to accept the invitation to the pulpit, Pastor Kirby had a conversation with me after the service. During the course of that conversation, he asked me why I did not want to be a preacher. I don't recall all the things I said to him, but I can tell you, following the course of that conversation, he assured me that I was a "marked man". He further assured me that I would not find peace in anything I did or pursued as a vocation until I accepted my calling to God's ministry. Subsequent to that conversation, my wife and I joined Greater St. Mark M.B. Church. In fact, Rev. Kirby baptized my wife when she changed her denomination from the Methodist faith to the Baptist faith. The church family became our church family. Until this day we have friends stemming from our introduction and connection to the Greater St. Mark M.B. Church. As a result of our joining Rev. Kirby's congregation, he became my personal mentor. He accepted me as his spiritual son. He was a graduate of Howard University and was the founder and organizer of Greater St. Mark M.B. Church. When the service concluded that Sunday, my wife and I left to return to my sister's residence where we were still living at the time. I believe we had about $79.00 between the two of us. My sister and her family had been eating up our food and destroying our personal belongings. Both of us were frustrated and nearly exhausted, so we decided to stop at Church's Chicken to get some food. After we had our food my wife said to me, "why don't we *not* go back home now?"

"I don't know anything about Detroit; where else can we go?," I asked.

"I don't know," she answered, "but let's just keep driving west on Eight Mile Road."

We came to the intersection of Telegraph and Eight Mile Road. Immediately after turning North on Telegraph Road we saw a tool and die company called Quigley Industries. There was a white man in the yard of that company picking up paper trash from the lawn. Just adjacent on the company's property was a sign that said "bench hands wanted". Immediately after my wife saw and read the sign, she said, "go there and talk to that man, you can get you a job!"

"Baby, you *know* I have never built nothing with my hands," I responded.

"That's alright-go there and talk to that man, he will give you a job!," she insisted.

Sure enough as instructed, I got out of the car and approached the man. I greeted him with the proper and appropriate greetings and he stood up from picking up paper from the ground. He returned my greeting with a firm handshake and eye-to-eye contact. He then asked who we were. He scanned our automobile and immediately saw it had a Mississippi license plate. I told him we were just coming from church, and that we had not been in Detroit for more than a couple of weeks; I was looking for employment and had just read his sign: "bench hands wanted". I told him I thought I could be of service to his company. Immediately he started asking who the lady was in my car. "Is that your daughter?," he asked me. I told him no, she was my wife. He then asked about my work experience and what I knew about tool and die equipment. I told him I had been a skilled pipefitter for Ingall Ship Builders in Pascagoula, Mississippi. He then said to me, "I am the superintendent for this company. My foreman's name is Mr. Esters. Take this note and give it to him by 9:00a.m. Monday morning." I said, "yes, sir!" then hurriedly returned to my wife in our car. She was happy and laughing, and then said, "*that* is why I did not want to go back there! Yes baby, we are gonna soon move! We're gonna get our own place!"

While we deeply appreciated our relatives allowing us to live with then temporarily, the experience was a rude awakening which quickly confirmed that people don't like you living with them in Michigan, even if it is for a short period of time!

I can say without a doubt, we experienced much pain and discomfort in the short periods of time we spent with our relatives. Now that I reflect on the times spent, I think the stays were deliberately made miserable so as not to permit satisfaction to enhance a short stay. The implied message was, *"don't get comfortable, because your stay is very temporary"*. Well, thank God, my wife and I soon got our own place shortly after I went to work at Quigley's, the tool and die company on Telegraph and Eight Mile Road.

As instructed, I reported to Mr. Esters early that Monday morning. I thought he would allow me to work with the crew of African Americans whose responsibility was to receive the dies once they had been used by the automobile industry. The company was organized into two sections. Once the rebuilt dies were distributed for use by the requested distributors, they were returned on a daily basis to be rebuilt again and again. This process was repeated over and over, because the company had a section that consisted of skilled and professional men who were well-trained and adept in using high-powered electrical equipment designed to cut out the defective parts of the punch press on a specific die. Now I thought Mr. Esters would send me to the group of African American brothers and sisters whose jobs were to unload the used dies off the trucks when they were returned from daily use. But Mr. Esters did not send me to work in the manual and routine labor. Instead, he allowed me to work with the skilled and professional trained men whose jobs were to operate the expensive and high-performing electrical machines to cut the defective parts from the dies so they could be reused the next day.

There were about fifteen professional skilled trained journeymen who were well-trained in using these high-powered machines. Mr. Esters' shop was situated so that he could constantly watch a man as he did his work in repairing his designated number of used dies. Each man was given no more than five dies to repair daily. I was hired on the job at a pay rate of approximately $9.89 hourly. I started to work on the job about the second week in September. Shortly after getting the job my sister's household started raising havoc and dissention, complaining why I didn't get jobs for them, since we had come to town and gotten jobs immediately. Well, jealousy and confusion got to the point where we had to immediately find ourselves a place to live peacefully.

CHAPTER TEN

We moved with my wife's sister and their family on Rosemont in Detroit. We stayed with them about two months. I kept talking to people I worked with, and finally, a co-worker told me about a one-bedroom apartment in Highland Park; it was a studio apartment located at 153 Ferris Street. We immediately contacted the owner of the apartment building, gave him the first and last months' rent deposits, and we were approved to get our own place. In the meantime, I was still working at Quigley's Tool and Die Company. Now to be quite honest, I never did learn how to master the high power electrical lace machines. The other fellas, my co-workers, worked diligently in an effort to teach me how to operate those machines. But the truth of the matter was two things: one, I was not gifted to be a skilled machinist, and the other thing, I had not been taught and experienced in that vocation.

After being on the job about three months and after many efforts by my co-workers to teach me how to operate the high-powered electrical machines—and also after messing up many of the used dies by not knowing what to do—the foreman Mr. Esters finally called me into his office. On my way to his office, the Holy Spirit spoke to me clearly and plainly: *"tell him the truth, because he already knows this is not your line of work!"* And after having reached his office, he called my name: "Thomas James McClellan, what do you do and who are you?"

I attempted to stall and filibuster to prolong the time, because I knew it was a moment of reckoning.

"What do you mean, Mr. Esters?," I asked.

"Thomas James McClellan, I asked the question to hear what you have to say now, because you have never built anything with your hands," he stated.

"Yes, sir Mr. Esters, you are right. However, I was trying to learn and I sure put forth a diligent effort," I replied.

"I know, Thomas, I have been watching you from the moment I hired you. You are a hard worker and you are a good man. But I cannot allow you to continue to come here every day and destroy the company's equipment," he told me. Now Thomas, you are a professional person."

"How did he know?," I asked him for the sake of conversation.

"I can tell by the way you talk and the way you write. Now tell me, what is your profession or vocation?," he asked. Then the Holy Spirit spoke to me and said, 'tell him the truth!', and so I told him I was a Science teacher by profession.

"I am going to allow you to work here until after Thanksgiving," Mr. Esters said. "In the meantime, the Board of Education for the employment of public school teachers is located at Putnam and Woodward Avenue in Detroit."

At the time Mr. Esters and I had this conversation it must have been early November, 1979. True to his word, he allowed me to work at the company until Thanksgiving. As he had instructed, I went to the Board of Education in Highland Park and Detroit and filled out applications for my specialization in teaching. My credentials had to be approved and sanctioned by the State Board of Education through a process of reciprocity, because I had previous teaching experience in the states of Indiana and Ohio. However, in the meantime, I still had to have employment in other jobs until I was issued a license to become a bona fide and qualified teacher by the State Board of Michigan.

I did a number of other jobs while I was waiting to be issued a Michigan teaching license. I recall succinctly, my credentials were approved and I was issued a license to teach in the Public School System December 12, 1979. While I was waiting for my credentials to be evaluated, one of the jobs I secured was as a security guard with Pinkerton Security Company. At that particular time, they were situated on Eight Mile Road just east of the Southfield

Expressway. Their pay rate was $3.25 per hour. I was working for them in the evenings and at night. My shift started at 7:00p.m. to 12:00 midnight. They sent me to Frazier, Michigan to guard a facility called a Remke plant, which made Coca-Cola trucks. In this particular company these trucks were made there and all of the parts were stored there. Frazier, Michigan at that particular time was not populated with many African Americans. I took particular notice of that fact shortly after I arrived at the plant's location. The guard shack was situated in front of the building about fifty yards away from the actual building. When I entered the guard shack, I found a small pocket New Testament Bible. When I opened it I immediately noticed written in its inside cover: *"This book will keep you from sin, or sin will keep you from this book!"* I thought after a minute to myself, perhaps somebody is trying to tell me something! Then I chuckled to myself, and quickly turned my attention to my new job assignment. With my new job I was not allowed to carry a gun. The company only permitted me to carry a flashlight, a watch clock with an inside tape. Throughout the building at specific locations were stationary monitors. When I made my rounds every hour, I was to go to these specific locations and insert the key for it to record the exact time on the tape in the watch clock carried on my shoulder. One particular Saturday afternoon about 5:30p.m. three young Caucasian males came to the work site. Now, I saw them coming in the distance; but the objects they had in their hands really disturbed me tremendously. One had a billy club in his hand, another one was dragging a piece of chain in his hand and the third one had his hands in his pockets. As I saw them approaching in the distance, a voice spoke to me clearly and said, *'don't allow them to get to the guard shack, go out and meet them'.* I greeted them with a big smile and a 'yes sir, boss-man!' Immediately the chain stopped making rattling noise, the other one stopped hitting his club against the ground, and the third one exclaimed, "nigger, where you from?" I said, "yes sir, boss, I am from Mississippi, what can I do for you all today?" One spit on the ground, rolled the tobacco in his mouth around and said, "nigger, we figured you ain't from here, because you know what to say to a white man. We come by here to get some tail pipes, some mufflers and whatever else we see we might want. But anyhow, nigger, we figured you ain't from here. Keep that attitude, ya hear? You'll live a long time, ya hear?" I said "yes sir, bosses!"

They went into that Remke plant and loaded tailpipes, mufflers, and other truck parts until they were satisfied. When the road supervisor came to check on me later on that evening, I told him about the incident. He then started to raise his voice to reprimand me, but before he could get started, I stopped him. I gave him all of Pinkerton's equipment, bid him a farewell, and dismissed myself from the premises. I told him he could forward me my final check in the mail.

The last job I had before teaching was for the Michigan Inn Hotel. I had a day shift working in the laundry. My supervisor was Mr. Richard Trice. He was an African American. He gave me and my wife a lot of nice towels and other items for our apartment in Highland Park. I had started to substitute teach for Highland Park School District since we lived in Highland Park. Immediately, Northern High School called me for a Science position. Mr. Crosby was the principal at the time, and he was also a graduate of Mississippi Valley State University. However, we were residents of Highland Park and I had begun substituting at Ford Middle School where Mr. Carl G. Pettway was the principal and Mr. Green was the assistant principal. I was teaching seventh grade Science and eighth grade Mathematics. I decided to stay with the public school district of Highland Park. The Highland Park Public School District superintendent was Dr. Thomas Lloyd, who came from

Coconut Grove, Florida. I taught at all the middle schools in Highland Park.

Immediately after becoming a permanent employee at Ford Middle School we moved from 123 Ferris to 249 Gerald Street. We lived there for only short while, then the last move we made in Highland Park was to 43 Florence Ave. Our residence was situated on the north end of Highland Park. Altogether, we lived in Highland Park for fifteen years. While residing there, I taught at the three middle schools that were located there. In 1988 State Representative Martha Scott became Mayor of the city; the school district and Mayor's office were interconnected in some fashion. At the beginning of the school year of 1988, I was transferred to Highland Park High School where I taught for a few months then Mayor Scott laid off about thirty-eight of us. September 1988 I reported to Cass Technical High School, whose principal was Ms. Jeanette Wheatley. I taught there one entire school year and at the end of that school year I was called into Ms. Wheatley's office for my evaluation. She invited me into her office by requesting that I pull my shoes off.

"Why do I need to pull my shoes off?," I questioned.

"Do you know who I am?," she replied.

"They say you're Ms. Wheatley," I answered.

"Young man," she stated, "I am Jeanette Wheatley, and I am supervisor over this specific district. I can fix it where you will not get a job here or any place in Detroit."

Well, I called her bluff, which is my way of saying I challenged her; I said I didn't believe she had that kind of power. She immediately ordered me out of her office. True to her words, that was the first and only time I taught in Detroit.

When I reflect on my entire teaching tenure in the state of Michigan, my teaching experience at Cass Technical High School was one of the most challenging and memorable experiences. Teaching in Highland Park has its moments as well, but I'd say my tenure at Barber Middle School presented the greatest challenge. Mr. Al Halper designated Barber Middle School as a magnet middle school. I am told he personally selected the staff and administration to work there. Unlike Ford and Ferris middle schools, Barber Middle School was host to Highland Park's brightest and best students. I had the opportunity to organize and set up the Science laboratory. The curriculum used science text books with the science labs connected to the daily lessons. The textbooks were structured quarterly, that is to say, they were sectioned to give a student three months of Biology with labs, three months of Chemistry with labs, three months of Physics with labs, and three months of Earth Science with labs. Consequently, the instructor could organize and create the laboratory geared to the subject matter of the students. I don't recall the specific year while teaching at Barber Middles School when we were competing in the state science fair. Subsequent to that year, the community of Highland Park came to my rescue. I attended a secretary's ball at the Book Cadillac Hotel in downtown Detroit, unannounced and uninvited. My popularity was already soaring in Highland Park because of my rapport with and effective teaching of the students in the community. My friend Mr. Charles Hanna, who is now deceased, was the resident manager at the Book Cadillac Hotel at the time. Charles was a friend to my wife and me, in fact he was our best friend. I met him through my wife during my early teaching career in Highland Park. At the time my wife met him, he was general manager at the McDonald's restaurant at Eight Mile and Greenlawn in Detroit. In fact, he gave my wife her first job as a manager. This particular McDonald's was owned and operated by an African American named Mr. Crumpler, who was married to a Caucasian woman, Mary. She was a sweetheart in character and disposition, and I learned so much from them as a couple. With their team effort and loving heart, I adopted a practice of non-resistance. Even then, I learned from the old man that you may not always agree with

152

another person's opinion, however, during those times you focus on the idea of non-resistance: an attitude of acceptance of what is—minus labels or condemnation.

Applying my spiritual gift of discernment, I learned to acknowledge that my opinion is just *my* point of view. And my prayer was not to change a situation I didn't like or the perspective of another person; but rather, to be aware of my thoughts, and to remember the spiritual truth of my being. That spiritual truth emphatically declares that I am one with the ever-present divine flow of a powerful energy source. Eternal events and situations have no adverse effect on the calm peace of my soul; consequently, with a loving heart, I always accept what *is*, as it exists. Ultimately, through the practice of non-resistance, I learned to receive gifts in every positive experience as I unconditionally accept moving through life with patience, faith, love, hope, and non-resistance.

The Crumpler family left an indelible impression on our marriage and life for years to come. Mrs. Crumpler was always counseling and frequently bringing other positive sister-women into my wife's life. Joann my wife continued her tenure at McDonald's restaurant even after the Crumplers sold their franchise on Eight Mile and Greenlawn and the one they had in Ferndale, Michigan. The last employment my wife had with McDonalds' was with an African American man who owned a franchise on Seven Mile and Outer Drive. His name was Napoleon Stewart. I was in my classroom at Barber Middle School when I received a telephone call from her; it was a distress call, I could tell by the sound of my wife's voice. Immediately, I reported to the principal's office to request someone to cover my classroom while I went to my wife's rescue. Sure enough, my wife was experiencing an episode with the owner, Mr. Stewart where he was attempting to take advantage of her in a manner that was not befitting to her character. As soon as I entered his store I went straight to him and requested an explanation.

Mr. Stewart had no plausible explanation for his behavior that was even remotely acceptable. Before I allowed him to attempt an explanation I took my wife out of his establishment and told him to take the money he had for her and ram it up his rectum. Of course you know, these were not my exact words. That was the last fast food establishment my wife ever worked for in Michigan. I brought her home and she and I had a series of conversations about future employment. After much discussion, she and I came to an agreement. I told her I would purchase a typewriter and teach her how to type. I purchased a Royal Academy electric portable typewriter with a disposable erasable ribbon. After purchasing the typewriter I also purchased a timer with a minute bell on it; the goal was to get her typing skills up to and beyond thirty words a minute. We worked faithfully and diligently until we accomplished that task. When my wife had met that goal, the next move was seeking employment at a bank—specifically, Standard Federal Bank in Troy, Michigan. The move that my wife made from the world of fast food restaurants to banking business in Michigan was precisely the right move to take her to the next level in her life. After she had prepared herself by acquiring and mastering the typing skill of thirty words in a timely fashion, she then searched the want ads in the local newspapers for an opportunity to utilize and apply her skills through employment. After diligently searching the want ads, she was fortunate enough to get an interview. We prepared for her first job in the banking business. When we arrived for her first interview, naturally she was anxious, but I kept reassuring, supporting, and encouraging her. We arrived about an hour before the actual interview. When the time came for her actual interview, we were greeted by a beautiful, tall and attractive African American woman named Ms. Deborah Bishop. Ms. Bishop was a God-fearing and devout Christian woman. She was the mother of two boys. At the time of my wife's employment she was also the manager at Standard Federal Bank in Troy. Ms. Bishop took my wife as a personal and family friend, and personally nurtured and mentored her in her job in banking; as a result of that employment opportunity, a family friendship was forged. Friendships were formed with at least three other ladies at Standard Federal Bank, and even to this day those friendships are yet sustained.

After about five years of employment at Standard Federal Bank, my wife decided she wanted to work for the airlines. When she came home talking about working for the airlines, I told her I was okay with the idea, except I did not want her to be a stewardess or flight attendant. She quickly assured me that she wasn't interested in that line of employment; she was interested in sales. I asked what specific airline she wanted to work for and she quickly responded that she was interested in working for Northwest Airlines, headquartered in St. Paul-Minneapolis, Minnesota. She knew exactly what airline she was interested in, and my response was to go for it. In her initial pursuit, she applied to several airline companies. Northwest Airlines responded favorably and selected her along with about fifteen other young ladies. At that time, I was completing my last year at Wayne State University so I told my wife to bring the other ladies to our home and study together in group sessions while they were completing their three-month course to qualify for employment with Northwest Airlines. My wife told me that twelve of them successfully completed the rigorous course given them. Consequently, those twelve were officially hired by Northwest Airlines and as I write my biography, my wife is still employed with Delta Airlines, which purchased Northwest Airlines about six years ago.

After leaving the Detroit Public School District in June of 1989 I was fortunate enough to become gainfully employed in August 1989 in the Pontiac Public School District. Prior to my employment in Pontiac, I had experienced an almost permanent employment opportunity in the Southfield Public School District. I had worked at both high schools in the Southfield Public School District in the mid-eighties. In fact, I had substituted for both Southfield Lathrop High School and Southfield Public High School. Mr. Cecil Rice was the general superintendent for the Southfield Public School District. The Southfield Public School District was very partial to employees from the Highland Park Public School District because Mr. Rice had once been employed there. As the story goes, Mr. Dan Hogan was principal at Southfield Public High School when the opportunity availed itself to me. Mr. Hogan was personable and likeable. In order to be considered for employment in the Southfield Public School District at that time, there were three interviews candidates were required to complete; several days of experienced substituting, and as many letters of recommendation as could be solicited from teachers were also needed. Now I must admit, I had no problems with the substituting experience. I had no problem getting letters of recommendation. I had a great rapport with the students I had taught for various teachers, regardless of the subject matter or area of specialization. The problem came on the third and final interview for the Science position at Southfield High School. This interview was scheduled to be conducted by the chairperson of the Science Department. The final interview was done at about seven o'clock p.m.; I believe it was on a Tuesday evening towards the end of the current school year. The principal of Southfield Public High School summoned me into his office. He reviewed a few major points he thought might be central to the interviewing process. After he and I had briefly reviewed those major points he finally concluded his remarks, stating he was certain I would do well. I was cautioned to be careful going before Ms. Joan Meyers, the reigning Science Department chairperson. I had seen Ms. Meyers on several occasions, even taught her Science classes and interacted with her students on numerous substituting occasions. Mr. Hogan and my wife had both given a word of caution. It wasn't that their words of caution fell on deaf ears; but I was a bit perturbed and perplexed as to what Ms. Meyers might throw at me during the interview that I wouldn't be able to handle. I thought that, as long as she dealt with my area of specialization, I had already hit a home run. Well, to my surprise, my wife and Mr. Dan Hogan had been correct. After about a half-hour into the final interview Ms. Meyers asked me the loaded question that resulted in my demise in ever getting a position in the Southfield Public School system. The loaded questions were: "What role has civil rights played in the acquiring of my education? What role had the civil rights movement played in me even getting the opportunity to apply for employment in the Southfield Public School District?"

Now, these were the two loaded questions asked of me during my final interview in seeking employment in Southfield. When I arrived home, my wife greeted me at the door. She said, "yes, honey I already know. You did not get the job." Mr. Hogan and I had already talked immediately following the interview. He knew before I reached his office. He said to me, "Thomas, had it not been for the civil rights movement and their contribution to this nation, you would not be allowed to visit the City of Southfield. Not to speak of living here, or even working here!" His final remarks were, "Thomas, perhaps in your leisure time you need to go to the library and read about Dr. Martin L. King and the many accomplishments that were gained because of his great sacrifice and many others with him."

When he was done talking to me, I felt so embarrassed, broken, and empty. But in the final analysis, I learned a lesson that will be with me as long as I am on the planet. Today, no one can inform me about the accomplishments and achievements of my people in American society; I can tell you, it was a lesson well-learned and one well-earned.

After that experience, I began employment at Pontiac Central High School in August 1989, and I continued teaching Science and Mathematics at both Pontiac Central High School and Pontiac Northern High School until June of 2000. My teaching experience in Pontiac was both bitter and sweet. My first teaching experience was at Jefferson Junior High School under principal Jimmy Randolph. I taught under his leadership for one year. The next year I was transferred to Pontiac Central High School. The principal there was Mr. Darryl Lee. A few years subsequent to my leaving Jefferson Junior High School, Mr. Randolph was indicted and convicted of child molestation. He was sentenced and sent to prison, and I was told by a reliable colleague that he'd died in prison.

CHAPTER ELEVEN

My experience at Pontiac Central High School working with the staff and Mr. Lee was very pleasant and enjoyable. Later on, I was transferred to Pontiac Northern High School. The principal was Dr. David Badger. Overall, I had excellent experiences at both high schools when the leadership were men. The public school system in the late 90s and early 2000s started to transition from the leadership of men to women, particularly in the office of principal. Personally, my bias is what I have learned and witnessed from experience. A woman is not a good selection to serve in the position of principal in high schools that are predominantly African American. Now, that leads me into the negative episode I experienced at Pontiac Northern High School with Mrs. Essie McGee serving as principal.

I taught ninth grade General Science while serving on her staff. During my first hour of the teaching day, I would start my class on time daily. I was not the type of teacher that was so regimented and strict that I assigned seats and specific rows. At the beginning of each school year, once I was assigned my classroom, subject matter, and grade level, I equipped my room to be inviting and appealing to the students. At the beginning of each school year, the first week of school was spent getting acquainted with the students, reviewing the rules for my classroom, and learning the names of the students. Rules and consequences were posted in an obvious location in my classroom. In addition, there was a poster board which read: "I hear and I forget, I see and I remember, I do and I understand!" My method of teaching was the affective approach; that is to say, I strongly believe in modeling the teaching of my students.

In my Science class, I had a young, out-of-control ninth grade Caucasian male. He had a problem with alcohol and marijuana. He was very belligerent, hostile, and disrespectful. He had no regard and respect for the principal nor any of the staff. He came to school whenever he felt he should, and when he came he was always late and under the influence of alcohol. I had talked with him on several occasions and attempted to find out why his behavior was generally so negative towards the school and staff. I noticed his disposition was totally against the school. This young man, whose name I don't recall, was totally out of control, and the principal Mrs. McGee turned an ignoring eye to his entire disposition and behavior towards Pontiac Northern High School. One Monday morning after several conversations with him regarding his behavior, he totally challenged and blatantly disrespected me. He came to my classroom door beating on it, and when I answered the door I questioned, "hey young man, why are you beating on my door?" About that time, he called me a big foot, Mississippi son of a bitch. In a knee-jerk reaction, I slapped him down to the floor. My next move was to really hurt him, but my male students hugged and restrained me by putting their arms around me. In the heat of the moment the young man, my belligerent student, ran away. The next thing I knew, after I had collected myself and calm down. Mrs. McGee was in my room asking what had happened. In the meantime, the young man who was the culprit had disappeared from the hallway and my classroom door where the incident occurred. Mrs. McGee never called me to her office to investigate the matter; when I looked up after collecting myself, the Pontiac City Police squad came and escorted me from my classroom after I had collected my personal materials and other school supplies. They were very cordial and polite. At least, they gave me ample time to get my materials and other personal belongings. The thing that I remember about the entire incident was the way Mrs. McGee had permitted the Pontiac City Police to come to Pontiac Northern High School and escort me from the school before my students, as if I was a hardened criminal. I will never forget the expression on my students' faces and the tears many of them cried that day.

That day will always have a special place in my teaching career as one of my saddest days in Michigan. There is nothing in all of my life experiences that I can quite equate to that moment of shame and embarrassment; being stripped of my dignity, honor, and professionalism in the presence of my students and colleagues. It will remain a day of infamy.

As time moved on and days passed, Mrs. McGee did not allow me to return to Pontiac Northern High School until the matter was addressed by the Judicial Tenure Commission of the State Board of Education in Michigan. The Judicial Tenure Commission sent a young attorney from the State Board of Education to the City of Pontiac to conduct a hearing in the community of Pontiac. The hearing started in March of 1999. The duration of this hearing lasted a week. This hearing was to be attended by my colleagues and parents of the Pontiac community. As I reflect on that dreadful week, none of my colleagues attended the hearing. Some of my students' parents attended. The facts were collected by the union representative, who was optimistic during the entire hearing. He had always told me it was a 'witch hunt' initiated by the principal of Pontiac Northern High School: Mrs. Essie McGee. He had also told me it was groundless and without merit for an indictment or a conviction, because the case did not have evidence to convict me. In any case, the hearing moved forward with several of my students' parents testifying to my teaching ethics and character in the community. Then about mid-week of the hearing came time for the young man in question to testify. He initiated his opening testimony before the young attorney by stating these words: "Mr. McClellan is the best teacher I have ever had. I have never had a teacher to teach me like him. Mr. McClellan is concerned about all of us, and he is fair to all of us. There is no way he would have done what he did to me, had I not made him do it."

At that moment the hearing was technically and literally over. Although it had been scheduled to last a week, they found other ways to utilize the next two days. Opening session for Thursday started about 11:00a.m. and was over at about 2:00p.m. The final day was Friday; opening session began about the same time it had begun on Thursday. At about 12:30p.m., closing proceedings were initiated. As the hearing moved swiftly to its conclusion, the young attorney called me to the witness podium. He began his remarks with praise and compliments on how pleased he was with what he had witnessed and heard for the entire week. Then abruptly, he ended his remarks with a question: "Mr. McClellan, given all that I have heard, and if you had it all to do over again, what would you do differently?"

"Counsel, I don't see anything I would do differently for two primary reasons," I answered. "It is my job as an adult and a teacher to provide an atmosphere conducive to learning at all times. Secondly, it is my job to provide safety and security to all of them as well."

Following and even during my remarks, the young attorney's face turned red, almost as a coal of fire. He made closing remarks and the hearing was adjourned.

As my wife and I were walking to our car, she said to me, "you know you lost that case, don't you?"

"Why do you say that?," I asked. "My union representative has assured me I have won this one, baby!'

"Baby, did you see the administrative lawyer's face and body language? I just want to prepare you; we will wait for his written verdict to come from the State Board of Education in about thirty days."

CHAPTER TWELVE

Sure enough, the written verdict came in the mail. And just as my wife had predicted, the administrative law judge ruled against me! Frankly, his verdict nullified any further employment for me in the city of Pontiac, Michigan; however, the administrative law judge did not forfeit my teaching license in the State of Michigan. Essentially, his ruling disqualified me from teaching in the City of Pontiac, but not in the State of Michigan. I took it upon myself to call the License Bureau for the Public School Teachers in Michigan. It just so happened an African American woman was the director. She pulled my license to teach in the State of Michigan and reviewed it thoroughly. Then she assured me with these inspiring and encouraging words: "Mr. McClellan, you will teach again in the State of Michigan because your areas of specialization are Mathematics and Science. For many years, there has been a crucial shortage in those disciplines, especially here in the State of Michigan. You will not teach in the City of Pontiac anymore. The reason I know this, Mr. McClellan, is because your license to teach in the state was not touched as a result of the verdict by the administrative law judge that handled your recent case in the City of Pontiac, Michigan."

For me, that was a breath of fresh air and a positive move toward restorative justice, and so a real ray of God's sunlight, hope and assurance flooded my soul. My wife had said to me when the incident initially happened, "Honey, for you to have knocked him down and dealt with him as you did, he really did something out of the ordinary to you. You really love children too much to be cruel and mean towards them."

Those remarks my wife made about me were not inaccurate in any shape, form, or fashion. My teaching tenure in the City of Pontiac and the County of Oakland ended in a way that left me with mixed emotions. I am sure there were students whom I left an indelible impression on their lives for years to come. Yet, there were others I left with the unanswered question: *why did it have to end this way?* On this journey called Life, I have learned that you take your experiences just as they are or however they come. These experiences that don't break you will ultimately give you a deeper insight, a stronger determination, and more resilience for years to come.

When I left Pontiac Public School District I was fortunate enough to get employed in a charter school in Detroit called Ross Hill Academy. Now, this school was established on the far Eastside of Detroit by the late Pastor W.W. Williams and his wife Mrs. Nellie Williams. I was told it was Mrs. Williams' dream to establish an elementary school and later an additional middle school and name it Ross Hill Academy. The school was birthed out of the William Chapel M.B. Church. The pastor was a good friend to my spiritual father, the late Rev. E.D. Kirby, the founder and Pastor of Greater St. Mark M.B. Church in Detroit. My first and only employment in a charter school was with Ross Hill Academy. Mrs. Williams employed me through Ms. Scott, the principal of her school. Initially, I was employed as a Science teacher. After working for a few weeks, Mrs. Williams discovered my skills in Science and Mathematics and how effective I was in teaching the children. She called me into her office one day and requested that I build a good science laboratory for the students. Mrs. Williams was the type of person who was very innovative and creative in working with children. Actually, I have no problems with that approach in methodology and technique; but in order to be effective in this approach, one has to be willing to spend a lot of money for supplies. Regardless of one's methodology in working with inner city urban children, there must be available monies to purchase the necessary supplies. Mrs. Williams was the type of employer who demanded the best from her teachers and staff for the children—but at the teachers' and staff's expense. I believe she was very pleased with my competence and ability as part of her staff; when the state administrators came to Ross Hill Academy from the State Board of Education in Lansing, she would come and get me to talk to them about the students and functioning of the school. One day she called me into her office and when we began to discuss why she called me in, she said, "Rev. McClellan, do you know you could make top dollar here?" As the conversation progressed, I asked her how that was possible.

"All you have to do just walk over the building and report to me what everyone else is doing," she replied.

"Mrs. Williams, I can tell you now, I will not do that," I stated.

Immediately, she became visibly insulted.

"Rev. McClellan, you will never have nothing!," she declared.

"Mrs. Williams," I said, "if I've got to get it by being a 'snitch', you are exactly right—then I never will have nothing. I will not do that, because that is not what you hired me for! You employed me to be a Science and Mathematics teacher."

At that point, she ordered me out of her office. Following that meeting, she cut my salary approximately three times before I finally left her school.

Ross Hill Academy had effectively become a middle school, which consisted of a day care center, elementary school, and a middle school. Mrs. Williams made sure I reported to her school at 7:30a.m. and I would leave at 6:00p.m. daily. The school did not provide adequate insurance or health care benefits for teachers. After we'd met and talked about what she wanted me to be—and I'd unapologetically refused her—she made conditions obviously difficult for me from that point forward. There was a young lady teaching seventh and eighth grade English at Ross Hill Academy, Ms. Shirley Adams, and she and I became acquaintances. While she and I were colleagues at Ross Hill Academy she would frequently say, "one day I am going to get better employment."

Shirley Adams was an exceptionally good English teacher. We often complimented each other on the skills and efficiency and quality of handling the students at Ross Hill Academy. Sometimes during the course of our conversations, she would jokingly say, "Mr. Mac, I am gonna get out of this place and where I go, I am gonna tell them about you!" I would respond by saying, "yes, Shirley Adams...I bet you will. You are gonna be too glad to get out of here yourself!", then we'd laugh and go on about our classroom assignments.

Sure enough, and as fate dictated the circumstances, Ms. Adams got the opportunity to be employed in the Inkster Public School system about six months before I was. She must have become a full-time employee for Inkster Public School District during the school year of 2000; the most significant part about the entire experience, she kept her word. Ms. Adams told her employer, Mr. Bland from the Inkster Public School District, about me. Mr. Bland called me following the completion of my first and only August Revival at my home church, Long Branch MB Church. My wife and I returned to Detroit after that revival on a Saturday evening in August, 2000. On that Monday morning about 10:00a.m., Mr. Bland called our residence. After our introduction, the first question he asked was if I knew Shirley Adams.

"Sure," I answered, "we worked together at Ross Hill Academy in Detroit, Michigan."

"Are you as good in Science and Mathematics as Shirley Adams says you are?," he asked.

I admit, it was difficult for me to remain humble; but as much as I could restrain myself under the circumstances, I managed to collect myself—and my exuberance, joy and excitement that Shirley Adams had kept her promise.

Mr. Bland extended the invitation to come to Inkster, Michigan for an interview and to meet Mr. Immanuel Wilson, the assistant superintendent. I accepted the invitation and subsequent to interview, I was employed by the Inkster Public School District in August 2000. Had it not been for Ms. Shirley Adams, I am certain I would not have gotten away from the Ross Hill Academy directed and operated by Mrs. Nellie Williams. Several public school districts had called there to verify my employment and even grant an interview for employment; however, I was told from a reliable source it was denied that I even worked there. I was astonished at Mrs. Williams' strange and unusual ways of making it extremely difficult for persons that did not conform to her requirements. She could make it personal if she deemed it necessary. It just depended on whether or not she valued the employee's worth at her establishment.

However, moving forward I was delivered out of the quagmire and the negative environment. I would be the first to admit that there were lessons to be learned in every situation I have encountered thus far. I believe the Creator allows us to go through this life encountering various kinds of experiences. While we are in the midst of these different experiences, we may not see or get the intended lesson until the saga is over. I have lived long enough to say that the Creator will not permit forward progress until the intended lesson is mastered; and so as I move forward, I frequently find myself thanking Jesus for the gift of forgiveness and life through Him. Through it all I have received joy, grace, love and fortitude.

The last ten years of my teaching career were spent in the City of Inkster, Michigan. When I accepted my assignment in the Inkster Public School District Mr. Immanuel Wilson was the interim Superintendent. Shortly after I began working a new Superintendent was employed by the name of Thomas Maridida. The district was soon taken over by an organization called Edison Public Schools. The first high school principal I worked under at Inkster Public High School was Dr. Cleaster Jackson. I believe Dr. Jackson was a native of Milwaukee, Wisconsin however, she resided in

Dayton, Ohio. The assistant principal of Inkster Public High School was Ms. Jan White.

Dr. Jackson immediately saw my worth and abilities in my areas of specialization, which were Mathematics and Science. She wasted no time in allowing me to work in my chosen fields of preparation. She immediately appointed me to the position of Chairman of the Math Department. Dr. Jackson was very impressed with my classroom management as well as my teaching ability in my areas of specialization. Within the next year or so after my employment in Inkster, Dr. Jackson appointed me the lead teacher in the Mathematics department at the Inkster Public High School. In conjunction with these promotions, Dr. Jackson reduced my classroom assignments and she began sending me to lead teacher conferences around the United States, sponsored by the Edison Public Schools. As you might imagine, a dispute was soon ignited between Mr. Wilson, who was acting Superintendent, and Dr. Jackson. Shortly thereafter, a disagreement started between the school board and Dr. Jackson. The dissension escalated to the extent where Mr. Wilson and the president of the local School Board eventually fired Dr. Jackson as principal of the Edison Public Schools. I never fully understood the business agreement between the State Board of Education of Michigan and Edison Public Schools, but I do know that the Inkster school board president, Mr. Rucker, and Dr. Jackson held an unresolved dispute. Consequently, that dispute caused Dr. Jackson's demise with the Inkster Public School District and the Inkster community.

After Dr. Jackson left Edison Public Schools, the Inkster Public School District was restored to a regular functioning local school district founded by the State of Michigan, like any other public school district. A new superintendent was elected by the Inkster community, Dr. Thomas Maridida. In my opinion, Dr. Maridida was the greatest and smartest educator I have ever met in an institution of higher learning.

The man was extremely competent, skilled, and qualified to function within the inner city school's brokenness and economic deprivation, caused by gentrification and other political moves by local government.

When Dr. Jackson—and especially Dr. Maridida—left Inkster Public Schools, I knew my days were short. Although I had planned to retire in 2012, when Governor Synder was elected he came in with a seeming vendetta against older public school teachers; he forced them into retirement by cutting older public school teachers' salaries in the name of 'union-busting'. He devised a law and forced it into the Republican legislature by giving older teachers a meager value on their pension benefits. With that meager benefit, older teachers were forced into retirement with restrictions that did not permit them to return to any classroom of any school subsidized by the State of Michigan. When the Teachers Union in the State of Michigan was forced to accept that law, it was a sad day in the state for many of its older teachers. Many veteran teachers were of age, but had not been in the classroom long enough for full pension and retirement benefits. Truthfully speaking, it was a curse and a benefit, depending upon where an older individual teacher was in the grand scheme of things. Then—as if that was not enough to digest—the governor swiftly returned to tax public school teachers' pension. Teachers whose birth year was before 1946 were exempted. Here again, fate favored my circumstances and teaching career in the State of Michigan. I am in my sixth year of retirement from the public school system.

I accepted my call to the ministry in August 1989 after having served three years as a deacon in the Hartford Memorial Missionary Baptist Church. My wife and I have been members of Hartford Memorial MB Church since I found it by accident on Thanksgiving Day, November 1986. I happened to be out driving in Detroit after having lived in Highland Park for seven years. At that time, my wife and I were members of the Greater St. Mark Missionary Baptist located on Grand River Ave. and Ohio Street. While Greater St. Mark MB Church had been the first church we joined after we relocated to Detroit, there were changes that were occurring in the congregation from the pulpit as well as the pews that prompted our search for another church.

Pastor Elmer D. Kirby had been instrumental in assisting and leading me in the acceptance of my calling in the Gospel ministry of Jesus Christ. There were changes occurring in Pastor Kirby's health. He had founded and shepherded Greater St. Mark MB Church from its inception to where they were when Joann and I found them. Pastor Kirby had been better than my biological father in encouragement, support, and compassionate understanding in accepting and nurturing my call to the Gospel ministry. He was my spiritual father. God, in His own timing and by divine providence, had guided me to the right person at the correct time regarding accepting my call to the Gospel ministry of Jesus Christ.

CHAPTER THIRTEEN

Pastor Kirby opened up his church to my wife and me. Though many of his members were receptive to us, many were resentful; however, they were not strong enough to deter Pastor Kirby's determination to mentor and nurture me in the infant stages of my calling to the Gospel ministry. Frankly, the relationship blossomed and developed into a spiritual son and father relationship that almost defies description.

Pastor Kirby became an integral part of our family structure to the extent that he was a viable and influential spiritual force in our lives. His presence and influence impacted almost every major decision that was made in our household. Frankly, his influence was so impactful I considered him a living and walking prophet. I say that, because he took a personal interest in our family, was our spiritual father and advised us in every way that affected our daily lives.

We were practically newlyweds, just a few months into the city of Detroit as a result of having relocated from the state of Mississippi. By sheer happenstance, we found Greater St. Mark MB Church because my wife was in need of a beautician. As a result of us seeking and finding a hairstylist in the Dexter and Linwood area of Detroit, the beautician who styled my wife's hair invited us to worship with her at her church the approaching Sunday. We accepted the invitation; and it just so happened the church was Greater St. Mark MB Church, whose pastor was the Rev. Elmer D. Kirby of Roanoke, Virginia, who attended divinity school at Howard University.

He was a very gifted, anointed, and knowledgeable preacher-prophet. I hardly know how to adequately describe how he managed to connect to my wife and me. Now that I have had ample time to analyze and reflect on our initial meeting, it must have been divine providence that brought us into the

171

fellowship and relationship of God's divine love and will. It never ceases to amaze me, even unto this day, how Pastor Kirby took me as his own son. I realize I was his spiritual son; but I can tell the world, we shared a spiritual bond and a divine relationship that was much stronger than that with my biological father.

As fate dictated the movement of our relationship and friendship, Pastor Kirby's health rapidly began to fail him in the 80s. Greater St. Mark Church's membership became fragile, particularly after Pastor's physical health began a rapid decay. Pastor Kirby's diagnosis was diabetes mellitus. This is a systemic disease; the effects of it can wreak havoc on its victim in a progressive way over a projected period of time. And so with the visible, rapid decline of Pastor Kirby's health, the loyalty and faithfulness of the church membership became stressed to the extent where the membership started to weaken and disintegrate. Some members left and went to other churches. However, those that were loyal and faithful to Pastor Kirby and Greater St. Mark's congregation stayed and served the declining congregation of Greater St. Mark MB Church.

My wife and I took a personal interest in the health and welfare of Pastor Kirby. The leadership of the church began to take care of him to a certain extent. Pastor Kirby had his own personal home on the East Side of Detroit on a street called MacDougall. His health deteriorated to the extent where he could no longer see and adequately take care of himself; my wife and I witnessed the abuse and cruelty heaped upon him at his weakest moments, health-wise. We had been in church meetings at Greater St. Mark MB Church and witnessed the venom and disparaging comments heaped upon Pastor Kirby—to the extent where he actually cried in open church meetings.

I can personally attest to the remarks he made to all of those who openly vilified and demonized him. He made predictions about their lives with the accuracy of death sentences; I am a living and earthly witness. Just as he predicted, they are all dead. Pastor Kirby was a very anointed and spiritually gifted pastor and prophet. I don't say these things about him because I knew his name; I say these things because he made predictions about my life and fate in the gospel ministry. Many of them have already been fulfilled in my life, and many of them are yet happening in my ministry and my life.

Divine destiny has a major role in all our lives. I have learned that some of us recognize its presence and others do not. By the time Pastor Kirby came into my life he was directed and sent by God. The things he did in my life, as well as my wife's, were by no means accidental; but they were initiated and set in motion purposefully for what I am currently doing.

That portion of my life was continued after meeting Dr. Charles G. Adams Thanksgiving Day of 1986. I happened to be out driving, surveying and getting better acquainted with the City of Detroit. As I proceeded to drive around the city, my travels brought me to the grounds of Hartford Memorial MB Church at 18900 James Couzens Avenue. I surveyed the beautiful designs and architectural structures of the magnificent building. I also noticed the amount of late-model and luxury automobiles. I was so awe-struck and fascinated by the scenery my curiosity compelled me to further investigate. I carefully found a safe park, and I went into the church.

After entering, I was welcomed by an usher and escorted to a seat in the rear of the congregation. Immediately I was awestruck by the preacher's message. The things that particularly grabbed me about this message was the power and presence of the Holy Spirit, and the delivery. While attending church was not out of the ordinary for me, what struck me particularly about this church and arrested my attention was its decorum, the atmosphere of its worship service and the church's etiquette. However, beyond its

173

uniqueness it was the power, delivery, and presence of the Holy Spirit that really caught me and even caused me to move up closer to the preacher.

The delivery of the message came forth with such a powerful anointing, the likes of which I had not witnessed before at any place in the city of Detroit. After the benediction, I went to this fire-and-brimstone preacher and introduced myself. He enthusiastically took my hand and introduced himself as Charles G. Adams. Following our brief introduction, he said to me, "you are a preacher, but you don't know it! Come join here, and I will help you."

Now, as you might imagine, I was shocked and in awe at such an announcement and prophecy over my life. Yet with all honesty and due respect, deep within my being I was not shocked. I had known for quite some time that God had a calling on my life to preach and teach His word through the gospel ministry, considering what Pastor Kirby had already set in motion in my life. Now that I reflect on the process of God leading me to Pastor Elmer D. Kirby and Pastor Charles G. Adams, both men had an important role to perform in the early stages of development of my ministry.

Pastor Adams has been more than an assistant and beacon of light in the shaping and developing of my current ministry. While I do occupy and have a professional title on his ministerial staff, just being present to serve in any capacity that I am requested is okay with me.

Currently, I am a member and sing in the baritone section of the Male Chorus. Let me further submit—as I would be remiss in my God-given duties of brotherhood and Christianity were I not to mention and give proper recognition—a male chorus called The United Voices in Christ. The group was formed in 1997. I began singing with the group in September 2005. I have sung with them for at least ten years. This group of men were organized and initiated by a brother named Mr. T.J. Adams. The group's origin has its roots in the Progressive National Baptist

174

Convention at the state's level. When it was organized initially, we were almost a hundred-man member male chorus. A fact that's even more fascinating about the group is that we were men who came from different church denominations throughout the Detroit metropolitan area. The United Voices In Christ's main mission was to give monetary scholarships to young men and women to assist them partially in tuition costs for the college of their choice.

The group is still thriving and singing songs to the praises and glory of God, though the group membership has reduced significantly. The last I heard, they are yet moving and recruiting new members, and still singing and praising our God.

I frequently attend Hartford Memorial MB Church's Wednesday night prayer service; occasionally, I am asked to preach during that service. Currently, I have six hours to complete in acquiring a Masters Degree in Divinity. However, I feel that at my age now, I am going to work in whatever capacity in the church and my ministry where I can best be of service to others.

As I envision the future and the many challenges that assail us as people, there is so much that needs to be done in advancing our people educationally, economically, and spiritually in God's church and in our world. I think we as a people are facing unprecedented and excruciating challenges unlike we have ever experienced—and all too frequently, particularly in the African American communities around this nation. I believe that those of us whom our Heavenly Father has equipped and prepared to make a difference, where and when we can are compelled to do so.

I have a ministry: "Returning Men to God Through the Church". My ministry was started in the year 2013, and our mission is: "promising a better life with God through relationship, friendship, fellowship, and discipleship". This ministry includes about a dozen other brothers and my spiritual son, Rev. Jamal Tyson-Bey, whom I discovered in my classroom while teaching a 10th grade Science class at Pontiac Central High School in 1993. Rev. Tyson-Bey is 30 years of age now, and well on his way in the ministry God has assigned to him. I still mentor him in his ministry and with other issues that he is frequently confronted with, being a young man of this generation. I have tried to teach him and others that Jesus Christ's primary ministry was to His father God for the sake of the world—*not* to the world for the sake of His father God. This means that the world's culture does not set the agenda for ministry, but the Father who loves the world and seeks its good sets the agenda.

The Christological or Trinitarian basis for ministry rules out utilitarianism—which tends to create ministry out of *needs* and *pragmatism.* As a result, it can transform ministry into marketing strategy. But God's ministry, through Jesus Christ's ministry, is always transforming, revealing, inspiring, challenging, and reconciling to man and God. Therefore, it links the church and the theological seminary in a mutual commitment to learning and healing.

Finally, as I bring my book to a close, I sincerely hope I have spoken with clarity, honesty, and sincerity in a way that transforms and directs someone to a ray of everlasting light that's available to any and everyone in search of it. I am becoming more and more aware over time that grace is the refinement of the soul.

Through time, I am convinced now that life is a menu; and I have learned from experiences that whomever and whatever I ordered for my life was delivered to my table. I am the sum total of everything I have ever seen, heard, eaten, smelled, been told, forgotten; it is all there. Everything influences each of us, and because of that fact, I try diligently to make sure that my experiences are positive. We may encounter many defeats but we must not be defeated.

Prejudice and bigotry are burdens that confuse the past, threaten the future, and render the present inaccessible. I have lived this life long enough to learn, unequivocally, there are few things more telling about a person's character than the small, unheralded gestures that highlight one person's kindness to another. I am referring to my best friend and fraternity brother Mr. Terrell Chapman of Memphis, Tennessee. His birthplace is Hollingdale, Mississippi, and we first met in Itta Bena, Mississippi on the campus of Ms. Valley State University in the summer of 1967. I have come to learn and accept his friendship is similar to that of a four-leaf clover: hard to find and lucky to have.

I remember during our years at Ms. Valley State University, he would often admonish me [by my nickname], "Jake, when you are always trying to conform to the mold others have for you, you lose your uniqueness, which can be the foundation for your greatness in life."

Now, as I take a retrospective look down the path of my life, I have concluded for myself that I am no better than anyone, and no one is better than me. My place in the world is no greater or lesser than that of anyone else. On that note, I close this book with a quote my mother taught me from the time I was a little fellow:

"If a job you've once begun, never leave it until it is done. Be its labor great or small, do it well or not at all."

UP FROM THE COTTON AND CORN FIELDS OF MISSISSIPPI:

A Photographic Overview

Our family home in the Long Branch community, near Durant, Mississippi. Standing on the steps is my cousin, John L. McClellan. On the porch, L-R is Mike Jones [RIP], my brother Albert L. McClellan, Jr. [RIP], and me. 1954

My parents, Mrs. Jannie Pempleton McClellan and Rev. Albert Lee McClellan

Our family

My beloved mother, Mrs. Jannie Pempleton McClellan, pictured here with my father's oldest sister, Beulah Weems

Mrs. Jannie " War Horse" McClellan
Dec. 25, 1902- March 8, 1984
Mama, That stick you put on us in the forties and fifties is illegal now, they call it child abuse, and that is a shame. You used to whip us so much, we called you War Horse behind your back. But, all ten of us are still living, and when I see none of us are in jail or prison, I always say the stick paid off.

We still love you Mama. William "Big Joe" McClellan and the rest of the family

The newspaper tribute to our mother.

My sister Inez's family: Mr. Bercy & Mrs. Inez Jones and their children Michael, Carolyn, Hyacinth, Melvin, Cassandra, and Marvin

My sister Lyneva's family: Mr. James & Mrs. Lyneva Gipson and their children Karen and Jacqueline

My sister Nannie's family: Mr. Will & Mrs. Nannie Fitzgerald and their daughter, Lynette.

My sister Causie's family: Mr. William & Mrs. Causie Cobbs and their children Derrick, Dedrel, and Cynthia

My sister Ora's family: Mr. James & Mrs. Ora Cain and their children Cedric and Jarrett

My sister Lena's family: Mr. Charles & Mrs. Lena Strange and their children Charles and Carl.

My brother and his wife, Mr. Eddie & Mrs. Hellen McClellan

My brother William's family: Mr. William & Mrs. Bertha McClellan and their children Phillip and William Jr.

*My family: Mr. Thomas & Mrs. Joann McClellan and our children
Terri and Kelly.*

*My brother Albert's family: Mr. Albert & Mrs. Ruby McClellan and
their children Albert, Kimitrea, and K-Sahana*

My cousin's family: Rev. Robert L. Holmes & Mrs. Gloria Holmes of Mt. Moriah M.B. Church in Waterloo, Iowa and their children Chondraah, Jawanza, Corey, and HaLanier.

"Success is to be measured not so much by the position that one has reached in life, as by the obstacles which one has overcome while trying to succeed."—*Booker T. Washington*

Philosophy of Education

Education is a life love and pursuit of knowledge and wisdom by intellectual means and moral self-discipline in a structured and organized way; using logical and rational reasoning in connection with empirical methods.

Mr. McClellan
Rm. #112

My life in the ministry

Ministry ordination ceremony, July 1992

My wife Joann and I.